DORIS JEAN'S
TRANSFORMATION

A True Story

How I transformed from a drug addict which I called myself a caterpillar to a beautiful woman who turned into a wonderful colorful butterfly who is a very genuine person I call myself a rainbow because I am full of color today.

BY DORIS JEAN WILLIAMS

DORIS JEAN'S TRANSFORMATION
A TRUE STORY

iUniverse books may be ordered through booksellers or by contacting:

iUniverse
1663 Liberty Drive
Bloomington, IN 47403
www.iuniverse.com
844-349-9409

ISBN: 978-1-5320-9188-9 (sc)
ISBN: 978-1-5320-9189-6 (e)

Library of Congress Control Number: 2020924733

Print information available on the last page.

iUniverse rev. date: 04/14/2021

A True Story

How I transformed from a drug addict which I called myself a caterpillar to a beautiful woman who turned into a wonderful colorful black butterfly who is a very genuine person I call myself a rainbow because I am full of color today.

CONTENTS

DEDICATION

God

EASY COME EASY GO

"I can do all things through Christ who strengthens me." He gives me the passionate desire, ability, and perseverance to complete this Book. I acknowledge my Lord and Savior whom all honors are due to Him.

To the late Rev. Joseph Lowery and his first lady Fannie Lowery whom were my grandparents always instilled in me to keep my head up and look to the hills from where my help comes from and to continue holding on to God's unchanging hands which was her favored song.

My oldest sister, the late Ola May Worthy Williams was a graduate of Kent State University of the nurses program in the 1970s when the killings of those students occurred. She told me that "You are one of the smartest people I knows." I just needed some tack at the time of my growing up years. One of the things that I have learned years ago is that having "Tack" is the way he or she speak or say something. I know she is looking down on me, and is proud of her little sister. I love and miss her so much. I lost my best friend in 2006 due to cancer.

Addicts: The sick and suffering addicts in the world who have the willingness as I did to change their lives, addicts of the world who are sick and tired of being tired of their diseases, the tireless pursuit to uncover the best in themselves, and once their best is found in themselves, they realize that there is a hero inside of them. There is a power greater than self. He or she has to want it, and may he or she find it as I did.

ACKNOWLEDGMENTS:

My Family: and Friends

I have to give special thanks to my old pastor, Anthony Johnson, "During many of my down times," he was there for me. When I went to Boot Camp, a prison program, I wanted our graduation ceremony to be different. Pastor Johnson sent me the words to "We Come This Far by Faith." I taught the song to my Boot Camp sisters, and we sang it at graduation with me leading the song. Pastor Johnson came to my graduation to support me. All my lieutenants could not believe he was my Pastor. I had the greatest gift of all. I thank you for all the support you have given me throughout my life and career. A true man of God.

Special thanks go to Ken Cash who gave me that extra insight on writing. He told me, that I have come a long way from when he first started tutoring me on my writing. I want to thank all the people who God has put into my life to make me see who I am. Without the help of him and God my book would have never got off the ground.

INTRODUCTION

In this book I am writing about events and issues as
they occurred and as I remembered them.

I started writing on this book of my life some thirty-five years ago when I was on one of my so-called vacations. A lot of my family and friends are gone to be with the Lord. Through the ups and downs in my life, I was told that in order for me to grow, "It all has to come out." My way was to write this book. My hope is to tell other addicts that change is possible. Never hold "Junk" inside you but find your way to get it out. You will find, as I did, that there are many people just like you, and like me.

God put it on my heart to get my story out there. I want to talk about how God put it on my heart to write my story. I have always said you never know who you will help by what comes out of your mouth. I have found myself helping so many people by my stories, experiences, hope, and strength. I wrote this during the three years that I was locked up. I remember every night the guards would come around and count late at night I would have woke up and went into the bathroom with the door crack and start writing. I was given special permission to go to the day room and sit at the table and write when I could not sleep. After getting home after three years, I went back 10 years later for a year. After getting out after three years, I stopped writing even when I went back to prison for that year. Instead, I went to Boot Camp because my life was a mess. I kept running back and forth in and out of the penitentiary. I did not know what to do with all the materials I had wrote while in jail until I kept talking to people telling my story, telling them what I did when I was locked up, people started telling me I should make another cope and get my story published. People started giving me names for the book. God started putting people in my path to help with my story. I have always had angles protecting me.

God my "Higher Power," continually gave me signals to straighten out my life and I ignored all of them, determined to do things my way. God came to me and touched my heart, I had the willingness within me. He let me know things had to change. I have to depend totally on Him. Today I am full of life, hope and determination. This story is my journey to wellness.

CHAPTER ONE

Life in the Ghetto, Elementary School Years And Being Sexually Molested

We were a family of eight: Mon, Dad my sister Ola, then Toris Jr who we call Sonny, then me, I am named Doris middle name Jean. After me, there is was my brother Michael, my brother Anthony who we call Tony, and my sister Teressa middle name Ann who we call Tress and she is the baby. Actually, I would add my mother's fourth daughter Barbara middle name Ann, who is really the oldest sister. We were a family that grew up very close together in our relationship. Mom made us children stick together. Barbara had a different mother and father.

Our childhood was happy and my years at Bolton Elementary School in Cleveland, Ohio were years when I was cute, delightful and impressionable. I played with my sisters and other neighborhood girl's. We played with our dolls, we played hopscotch and we played hula-hoop. My mother kept my long, jet-black hair tied in ponytails or braids, with ribbons or barrettes. However, I really wanted to be a boy.

I climbed trees, played ball with my brothers, and raided the neighbor's fruit trees. We would come home with a bag full of grapes, apples, or my favorite, cherries. Deep, dark red, they were ready and very sweet. With my brothers, things were exciting. However, they complained that I was a girl, easily hurt and start to cry. They tried to lose me by going through short cuts, brushes and running through trails, I got tired and went on back home.

I got very tired of my hair, so I cut my hair off with scissors. When my mother came home from work that evening and saw my hair, she beat me. My hair grew back, longer and prettier. Then I cut my hair off a second time and then a third. The third time I cut my hair I used electric clippers that were used to cut my dad's and my brothers' hair. My hair never grew back the same. Although I did not realize it at the time, I was hardheaded then until I got much older. If my mother told me to walk down the street, I had to run. My mother really was thinking I was crazy or had a mental problem. No one understood me so I thought. She kept me at the doctor's office for one reason or the other. My mother took me back to the doctor when I had suddenly lost a lot of weight. The doctor had seen me only six months before and was sure I was not the same girl. Therefore, my mother told him that all I had been eating was dill pickles and a candy cane in a lemon. We lived in a nice neighborhood on a clean, neat street. At the end of our street was a swimming pool. On hot summer evenings, as most of children in the neighborhood would jump the fence to get to the pool. However, I was teased for being heavy, calling me "Pig" as I climbed over the fence. Therefore, I devised my own diet. I was about ten years old, my parents used to say, "They knew all their children and what they would do, but they were ever so wrong. Mom was somewhat right sometimes. At this time, there were only four children. My mother had two girls and two boys. My oldest sister, Ola May, was always the dainty little girl that hated to get a spot of dirt on her clothes. Times were hard back in the 60s when I grew up. I remember I had a lunch card and my friends did not; that was embarrassing to me. My father worked for a factory named National Mauve in Cleveland, Ohio, which was in walking distance from our home. He had a bad drinking problem. When he came home drunk, he wanted to jump on my mother. Well, we as small children, got tired of looking at our mother cry. One-day Daddy came home with the same old ways of him talking very foolishly wanting to jump on our mother. My sister, Ola was the oldest in the house. She did nothing but cry; my brother, Sonny, had the bat, I had the broom, and my brother Michel had the mop. As he started beating Mommy, we started beating him. I was yelling, "Leave Mom alone." Well, he had finally realized that his children were growing up and were not going to tolerate him beating mother anymore. Shortly after that, he stopped. If the beating continued, we children did not know anything about it. We were living in the heart of the ghetto, on Cedar Avenue off East 100 St.

The six of us and Jean is in the middle

I was always heavy as a child. I got tired of my sister, Ola, and my two brothers calling me a pig all the time. If they were not calling me "Piggy," it was Oink, Oink or Fatty, so I wanted to lose weight so badly and I could not. I really did not know how at the time. I used to love eating a candy cane with a lemon. I would dig a hole in the top of a lemon. Then put the candy cane in the middle and suck the juice out; it was very delicious. It tasted like a sweet lemon and a peppermint. I ate that along with a big kosher dill pickle when I was a child. At that time, the cost for both was twenty-five cents each. I do not remember how long I ate this, but I do know I lost weight fast, fast enough to make my mother think something was wrong with me. She took me to the doctor who I hated because the doctor had that plastic thing that looked like a big "Penis" that was used to go up in girls. By me being a young girl, I was ashamed to let my body be exposed to anyone. This doctor was our family doctor; he told my mom that "She is a very strong girl." I had said it was baby fat. I told my brothers, "You all cannot call me Fat or Piggy anymore. Now I can really keep up with you all." I was big for my age and I looked older than I was. In the summer, we loved to play soft ball in the backyard with some of the neighborhood children. Both of my brothers knew I had a habit of hitting the ball and then throw my bat. All the children who played with us knew it as well. They said, "Look out; Jean's at bat. Mom used to warn me about that all the time, it just seemed like I could not help it. One particular time, my brother, Michael, was the catcher. My brother Sonny was pitching the ball to me. I hit the ball and threw the bat, then took off running. The bat flew back and hit Michael in his forehead. The impact knocked him out. He was lying on the ground, lifeless in a pool of blood. I said, "Oh God, I have killed my brother." I started hollering and screaming. My mother ran out of the back door to see her son lying there lifeless. She called the ambulance. They came right away. In the meantime, she was putting cold towels onto his forehead. Well, she was too busy with him to ask what had happened. I cried and cried. Not only did I know I was going to get the living shit beaten out of me, but he was my brother and I did not mean to do that. I got my ass beaten so much for that; however, I kept throwing my bat. He went to the hospital; they fixed him up and let him come back home. While they were gone, I was crying my eyes out because I knew when Mom found out that I had swung the bat and it had hit him in the head, I was doomed. I wanted to hide somewhere, but I could not. I felt the accident was not my fault because everyone knew to get out of the way when I hit the ball. That is how selfish I was, and I did not know I was at the time. Sure enough, she beat me so long and hard until I thought she was trying to kill me. I did not hit another ball for a long time after that. I used to sit on the back porch and watch them play. My brother, Sonny, always made fun of me about the accident. I did not see that incident as being funny, and I used to get very angry. In return, I made fun of Michael. I told him he could not talk about anyone, Ha! Ha! Ha!" .My sister, Ola, was too pretty to play ball with us. She always wanted to play with her baby dolls. Then there were things coming up missing a lot, money, mostly. I used to tell my parents that I had taken whatever was missing because no one would say who really stole the missing items. They always held back because they knew after we had gotten whooped a while, that I would admit, I did it, and I left it at school. My mom used to say every time to bring it home the next day. I would say, OK. The next day I would not come home. I went over to one of my mother's friend's house, Mr. Buddy, which is what we called him. He was the only one at the time I could think of. He lived around the corner from us, on the corner of 100Th Street and Cedar Avenue.

At the age of twelve, I ran away from home for the first time, but not my last. Mr. Buddy asked me, "What were I doing out that time of night?" I was crying. He told me to come inside. He kept asking me why I had run away. I finally told him. I told him about all the money coming up missing at home, and I always was blamed for everything, and I was tired of it. I did not know how to fix it. At the time, I did not know that all I had to do was to tell the truth and stay with the truth, no matter what. He lived in an apartment building over a restaurant. He went downstairs to the restaurant and got me a cheeseburger with french-fries, along with a soda. I begged him to let me stay. I said, "Please Mr. Buddy, do not tell Mom that I am here because I never want to go back home." What I did not know was that he called Mom anyway, and she picked me up the next morning. He had only a one-bedroom apartment. He put me on the couch, and then he went and got me some covers. It was summertime; all I needed was a sheet to cover up with. He said, "Here is a tee-shirt, do not sleep in your clothes." I said ok! Little did I know that he was not about the right thing by me. Mr. Buddy was a real nice man or so I thought until I was blackmailed by going to bed with him. He was my mother's friend. He came over to our house and took my mother and us children places. He also bought us things, and he was always giving me money; therefore, I trusted him. While I was eating, he went into the other room, called my mother, and told her I was there at his place. He also told my mom he promised me he would not call her because I was very scared and shaken up, so mom agreed to let me stay over there all night. In the meantime, after I made up the couch, he came into the living room to talk to me until I fell to sleep. He was still being nice to me. He asked me questions about boys I went to school with and things like that. At the time, I told him that I hated boys because they were bad and they used to "mess" with me all the time, because I had long jet black hair. The boys used to pull my braids all the time and I would get very upset at them. I asked them, "Why you guys just cannot leave me alone?" I would fight them all the time.

He waited until I was good and asleep, and he raped me. I did not know exactly what to do or say. I asked, "What are you doing? "Get off me!" He asked me if I was a virgin. I said, yes. He then said this will not hurt and it did. It hurt real badly. Then he started playing with my undeveloped breast. Then he reached over onto the table and got something, a safety device. He took it out of the package and slowly put it onto his penis. I just laid there watching him saying to myself, "Oh God! Do not let this man hurt me!"

I will never forget that because I felt that I had brought that on myself; however, I was a child and I did not know. After it was all over, he put me back onto the couch. He gave me some money and told me not to tell my mother about what had happened because she would not believe me. He also said that I did not have anything to worry about because he would take care of me from that point on. I was hurting in my private area. I was feeling really badly, dirty, and I did not understand why I was being punished. I figured it was because I was so bad and hard-headed. God was punishing me for running away from home. The next morning, I awakened with a knock on the door. He answered it. It was my mother. She was standing in the doorway to the apartment. The living room was right there by the door. I jumped up off the couch and said, "Oh God!" I said to Mr. Buddy, "You promised me you would not call my mom." He said, "Jean, your mother would have been worried about you all night."

I was feeling stupid, as if he had set me up for this, to take advantage of my body, to take my virginity. I cried and cried; however, I never said a word to anyone. I was very scared after that. I really did not know why, meaning when things did not go right for me at home, Mr. Buddy was always there for me. I did not know any better; I was a child. He took advantage of me. My mind told me that he was not going to keep on raping me repeatedly. How could I expect a different result, when I kept running right to him every time I ran away from home his logic worked, because every time after that when I ran away, I would go right over there to him, knowing what he would do to me. He would rape and feed me. He talked me into going back home without telling my mother. Mom had gotten to learn my pattern. When I ran away I never did approve of what he was doing to me. All I remembered is that it used to hurt so badly. I really do not know why I continued to let him do those things to me. As time went on, I got more and more afraid to tell. I let the situation get very out of hand instead of telling someone when it had first happened. I had no idea it was going to lead up to what it did; now I really do not understand the situation anymore. I kept it bottled inside of me for many, many years., Mr. Buddy would be the first one mom would call. However, he would say, "No, I have not seen her."

During my junior high school years my favorite hobbies were sewing and cooking classes. I took home economics in the seventh grade at Rawlings Junior High School in Cleveland, Ohio, on East 79th Street. That was a very bad year for me because I was in special education classes where I stayed in one classroom all day. I did not like that. In cooking classes we learned how to cook some very interesting dishes such as homemade cookies, candy, broccoli with white cheese sauce and many other things. Boy-oh-Boy! That was the "bomb." It was mouthwatering good! The best part of it was that we got to eat everything that we made. There were two guys in the class who wanted to learn how to cook. I admired them because who is to say that they would always have a woman around to cook for them. I also took up sewing. The first thing I made was an orange stuffed animal it was a turtle. I was in the Glee Cub as well. Singing was fun to me as well; I love singing even although I could not sing that well; however, I could blend my voice with others very well.

Mom was thinking about buying a home in Garfield, Heights, Ohio. She took us all to see the house to see how we liked it. It was a nice, big, fine house with nice grass in the front and backyard. The house had an upstairs with three bedrooms and a huge living room with a fireplace; it had a dining room, and big basement. My siblings and I were so pleased with the new house where we would be living It did not matter to Dad, because he was a simple man who did not ask for much.

Dad had gotten hurt on the job in 1966, and he could not work anymore, so Mom said that it did not make sense to continue staying where we were, because her children did not have grass in the front or backyard. We also had to share a house with the people upstairs.

My parents had struggled with their children so long and hard at that time. We did not have the best of things in life; however, my mother kept us all clean and fed. As Mom told us all the time, it was hard times in the 60s, especially for a husband and wife with hardly any education. My parents wanted to get us out of the ghetto, into a better environment and a better school system.

Our new house was so big and pretty. My siblings and I had better and bigger bedrooms. I was a happy child to move to a brand new neighborhood. The new school I went to was better because I did not know anyone; it was a better part of town, and most of all we were out of the ghetto. My new friends there were much better because they were not about violence. I was in the eighth grade by then, starting at Jamison Junior High. We moved into our new house during the summer.

CHAPTER TWO

Junior and Senior High School

I was now thirteen years old. The school year came about Mom enrolled us into our new school. My oldest sister, Ola, was a senior at John Hay High School. My oldest brother, Sonny, was in the tenth grade at John Hay. Ola wanted to graduate from John Hay with her friends. Mom left her there, and Sonny stayed on with her so she would have someone over there with her. After Ola graduated that next year, Sonny went to John F. Kennedy High School. I was in Junior High School at Robert H. Jamison. I felt as though I was the happiest child that had ever lived! I said to myself, "Now the rapes will stop. Now I will be where no one knows me." It would be a new start, and a new beginning, on the other side of town. I was so, so very happy!

I was very active in school. It took me a very long time to like and trust boys. I was in the eighth grade and I wanted to be a cheerleader. I had an older cousin at Jamison Junior High School named Jackie; she was in the ninth grade, my cousin worked with me that entire summer at my new house in my backyard to learn to be a cheerleader. She taught me how to do a "Round off" which was the hardest task for me. She taught me how to flip correctly, do splits, summersaults and some of the routines that the cheerleaders were already doing.

School started that September of 1969. I tried out for cheerleaders. We had about two weeks or so to practice. I felt I was on top of everybody else. We had tryouts and I made the team. I made Junior Varsity! I was so proud of myself. Now I was glade about all my hard work. I had a lot of confidence that the next year that I would make Varsity and I did. Now we were doing harder cheers, flips, spits, and rounds-offs. It was a lot of hard work, but I enjoyed every bit of it. That was the greatest pleasure for me, to be a part of the team.

In that particular year, word had gotten out around school that a group of people was coming to the school, and everyone who did not have an Afro hairstyle was going to get beaten up. All the Black girls were in the bathroom washing their hair with soap, including me, to get the hair napped. I was so scared! This hairstyle was for Blacks back then. Usually the hair would turn soft and fuzzy. The groups of people made all the girls look bad because they never showed up. I never knew how that rumor got out. Now I had to go home and explain to my mother why I was coming home with nappy hair. My mother thought that it was very funny. I did not think it was funny at all because I was really scared and was ready to leave the school right then, but it was said that as long as we had something that looked close to an Afro, the group of people would not mess with us. Well, I guess that was a big joke, but I thought that joke was not funny.

By this time, boys were looking at me, and I had started to like boys, but I was still very scared of them and no one knew why. I finally did get a boyfriend, and I was very scared to kiss him. There came the point in our relationship where I trusted him a lot, and he promised me that he would never hurt me. Well, of course, I still did not believe a word he said. All he wanted was for me to go to bed with him. He came to my house a lot, and my mother started liking him. She said he was a very nice young man. No one really knew all that I had been through at an early age. To tell the truth, I was glad to get away from Cedar Avenue. I figured I would have a new start on everything, where no one knew me. It was a new beginning for me. I had stopped being raped; however, the damage had already been done to my body.

My boyfriend always said to me that something had happened to me in my life very bad that I did not want to talk about. I asked him why he said that. He said it was because I was so withdrawn from many things he tried to do to me. He said it was because I was scared to be touched. I said to myself, "How did he know I had been raped?" I just shrugged it off and said all this is new to me.

As time went on he was very patient with me, and he brought me out of my shell. I remember the first time I did have sex with him, I started talking very crazily. It made him scared, and he kept asking me about the situation and continued to take his time with me, trying to find out what had happen to me in my life. I kept on saying nothing. Then he asked me if I had ever been raped. I said "No. Why are you asking me that? "He said, "You are so scared!" He said that when he put his penis into me, I was shaking. I know he did not believe me. He knew I had been raped. I threw the rape out of my mind altogether. I did not want to think about the past. I was glad that I was away from it all. I did not want to ever think about that situation again in life, although I think it was still in my subconscious mind, because I would see things on the news and talk shows where girls had been raped and it affected my thinking about men..

As I grew up, it did not affect me in any kind of way, or so I thought. I just used to say, "That is a shame," especially if it was a child that was involved. I always thought why does a man have to rape young girls or babies? I now know it is because they are vulnerable, but I did not know that back then. Sex comes a dime a dozen. A woman will give it up most of the time if a man finds the right woman. The woman will sometimes give up sex for money. I do not understand why a man has to take something that is not his. All of the nice things in life which I had then still did not stop the money from coming up missing. I thought I was losing my mind. I really did not think I was going to live to become an adult. My running away from home did not stop. Things got worse. More money came up missing.

When I was about fourteen years old, I remember this one incident: my father told me to get in the bathroom buck-naked. He thought he was going to beat me. He did not know that there was no way I was going to allow that to happen because I was a fully developed young girl. Well of course, I thought he had lost his mind. I was not going to get buck naked to go to the bathroom and wait for him to come in to beat me. I was in the bathroom sitting on the end of the bathtub thinking what was I going to do when Dad opens the door? I said to myself, I have to get out of here, he will have me cornered. When he opened the door, I caught him by surprise, off guard, and rammed him like a football player. I mean to say that I hit him hard because I was scared. I pushed him into the wall outside of the bathroom. He stumbled and fell. I ran down the stairs and out the side door. After I got outside, Dad was right behind me yelling for me to come back. I slammed the door so hard that I broke the glass. Little did I know, at the time, the glass had cut me. I did not know where I was going. It was about 9:30 p.m. The street lights were on. When I got under streetlights, I saw the blood on my blouse; I started hollering at the top of my lungs, "Momma, Momma." At the time I did not know where the blood was coming from so I ran back home. When my parents saw me, Dad had forgotten about the beating. I kept saying to my mother that I was dying, she said, "No you are not. Stop crying and let me see where the blood is coming from." She took me upstairs to the bathroom and washed the blood off my face. I could not stop crying. Finally, she saw a cut under my right eye. My eye could have been put out. I started screaming, "Daddy did it. He tried to put my eye out! My mother kept telling me that my Daddy did not try to hurt me; she said "Jean, you broke that window yourself." Mom just kept on telling me that until I believed it. I begged Mom not to take me to the hospital. Mom knew how I felt about doctors and hospitals. She felt that the cut would not heal correctly, because it was very close to my eye. I told mom that she could fix the cut. She did, and the cut healed up very nicely. If Mom thought the cut was that bad, she would have taken me to the hospital anyway regardless of what I said. My skin always developed keloids when I got cut. That is why there are so many concerns about me when I get hurt or cut, and I was always getting hurt. I was very clumsy and accident-prone. My father forgot all about that beating.

It was time for me to graduate from the ninth to the tenth grade. This meant I was getting ready to go to senior high school, and I was so scared. I thought, the big bad people are there! It is time for me to really grow up now. I felt like I was improving in life. We had started preparing for graduation. We had rehearsal on how to walk and march in. We were just going over the routine of how it would be on graduation day. The rehearsal for glee club was very exciting to me, to sing at my graduation. Therefore, it was finally that big day for us ninth graders. All of my family was there. We had on white blouses and black or dark skirts with black or dark pants. I will never forget that day because I was in the Glee Club as well; I had to wear a navy tam on my head but only to sing in. My brother, Sonny, was taking me to school that evening which was during the winter months. By me having to sing, I had to be there a little early, so my father told my brother Sonny to take me. But he did not want to drop me off; he said that was going out of his way. My Dad told him that I was not going to walk. If he did not have the time to drop me off; then he could not go where he wanted to go. He was very angry about my father's decision. He was very upset with me. As we got closer to the schoolhouse, he went down a side street that was directly in front of the school. We did not quite make it to the school because we got into an accident. He was trying to go too fast and slid into a parked car. I thought the world had ended. I was very shaken up but it was not that bad. I did not know to whom the car belonged to but the people came outside. I was crying. Sonny told me to shut up I said "I am going to walk to the school to call Mom and tell her what you had done".

All those problems I went through as a child. No child should have to endure those experiences. Sometimes I thought I had brought most of my life's problems on myself. After I lost all that baby fat, I looked much better. Sometimes I thought that I grew up too fast. I was built like a brick house. I always had low self-esteem. Today, I have overcome that problem.

Because I was a slow learner, there were things in life that I thought I could never do. I would never try to do things like taking chemistry, art, or any hard classes because I was afraid of the challenges. What I did not know was that I was defeating myself before I started.

The younger generation of today is missing so much. Children, teens and young adults should try to stay in their places as long as they can because it is not going to be as easy as he or she thinks. The world is mean and quarrelsome; young people should stay with the winners. Young people of the world today are growing up too fast. Children of today are missing their childhood because either they are having babies too young, when they are only babies themselves. They want to get fast money by selling drugs, which will only lead them to jail. This will make them have a felony record. That is the biggest mistake he or she can do because take it from me, once in the system, it is hard to get out. It is a label or a number that will follow you throughout life. I hate my past; however, it has made me a much stronger person today. After being in prison three times, I finally understand, crime does not pay. I tell all young people to get an education while you are young. Robbing, killing, stealing, or doing wrong is not right. Like I was once told, "Doing wrong, you will get paid back, and you will get it before you leave this world." Just when a person thinks he or she is doing so well, there comes a setback to make you think, why me Lord, why me? However, you brought that on yourself. You had better believe the Lord is sitting high, on his throne, looking down at us all. He knows it all. I feel sometimes today that I am still being paid back for all my wrongs. You cannot fool God; you are only fooling yourself. When a person had done something to me, I had to pay him or her back; however, I had no idea as to how to get back at a person for wronging me. I used to hold grudges on people and was very revengeful. It could have been ten, twenty years from the time in which I was wronged. Often that person would have forgotten what he or she had done to me. Thank God, He has finally taken those evil thoughts out of my mind, body, and soul. Now, today, I do not seek revenge. I put it into God's hands and let Him handle the situation. It was hard for me to learn from my mistakes. It is still hard for me not to worry about things in my life because I am a worrier. Today, I am working on that situation, and I have come a long way with God's help. Negative things in life and negative people stop growth. Growth is what life is all about. Who wants to continue going around in circles the rest of his or her life? I do not think a person who wants something in life will do that: it may be that revolving door that he or she does not know how to change.

I had been raped at an early age; I did know what an orgasm was until I was with my boyfriend, Dennis, from Jr. High School. He was thinking I was a virgin. I never had experienced an orgasm. Dennis kept telling me that the feeling would come again. I asked "When?" He laughed. That feeling did not come back that day. Dennis stayed with me mostly all day. I just could not get over that feeling; it felt like a big explosion of energy that was being released inside of me. I will never forget my very first time. It was very special to me. He and I stay together through junior high school. We had fun for the rest of the summer. Today he is dead.

Summer had gone. Fall had come. I was in senior high school at John F. Kennedy High School as a tenth grader. We were called "Flats." The first day of school, the kids seemed so big and so did the school. I was so scared! I was assigned to my homeroom and classes. I had to report to each class throughout the day. I started meeting some of the other students that I had classes with. I never have met people easily because I was so shy. I did not like to talk, I got in trouble a lot and, I liked to fight. My boyfriend Dennis and I broke up when we got to senior high but we were still friends. He got involved with the wrong boys; shooting up drugs, popping pills and whatever other drugs he could get. I had to leave him because of that. Another boy named Fox was interested in me. He was cute. All the young ladies wanted him. I wanted to talk to him anyway, but I was scared and did not know what to say to him. Fox knew that I was very shy and quiet but that did not stop him. He kept after me until he got me. We had a very good relationship. Every time others saw him, they saw me. All during high school, when we got out of school for the day, we usually were together. We had a very good relationship. In school, we stayed in the "Recreation center" dancing. I cut classes to stay in the recreation room dancing for 4th, 5th, and 6th periods. I loved to dance and so did he. He, I and some other friends used to practice hand dance steps. Many people said that Fox and I looked like brother and sister, we were just that close. We used to cut school to go to other high schools' recreations centers to dance. That was some of the fun for us back in the 70s. I loved sewing ever since Junior High. Sewing was my best class. Most of the time, a person could find me in the sewing room or the recreation room. I did just enough with my other classes to get by. In the 11th grade, I did not cut classes at all.

Later, it was time for cheerleader try-outs. I wanted to be a cheerleader since I had been one in junior high. I thought I should have made the team with the other cheerleaders who came from Jamison with me. I was so disappointed because I did not make JV. I had worked very hard. I considered myself just as good as and better than some of the girls who made the team. I guess I was not pretty enough, did not know enough people, and was not popular, or so I thought. I had very low self-esteem. I was just as pretty as other girls, but I did not know it. I thought the judges were playing favorites. Then I tried out for High Steppers who were called the First Ladies. My girlfriend and I tried out for the team we were in the same homeroom. High Steppers had two tryouts. My girlfriend and I made the first tryouts. During the second tryouts, I was so nervous, but thought I had done a good job. I really thought we had both made the team. The judges brought a red flower to each girl who made the team. As the judges were walking down the hall they only had one red flower. We both were wondering which one of us had made the team; it was her. I was upset again, and angry at the world. I vowed I will never try out for nothing else at Kennedy. I never smiled much. People used to think and say that I looked angry all the time, but I was not. My boyfriend, Fox talked and talked to me. I did not care; I really thought I was a loser.

I got more and more into my sewing, I knew that it was something I was very good at. I was one of the best sewers in the 11th and 12th grade. I knew who could do what in my sewing class. My sewing teacher would sometimes let students stay in for 4th, 5th, and 6th period, which were the lunch times. At times, she cut back and ran all students out because she knew sometimes we were lying. If a student really had study hall, then it would be all right to stay. My best girlfriend Shelia and I were in sewing class together in the 10th and the 11th grade.

I found out that the high schools were having a sewing contest. Our school had won this contest for the last past four years. This sewing competition was only for seniors. Boy-OH-Boy! Here I go again. How I would kill to be the one to represent our school! My sewing teacher did not have anyone in mind for the contest. I wanted to be the one, so I asked her. I was just a junior. I made my prom dress a year early. It was a very beautiful dress. I had to beg and beg Ms. Smith to let me represent the school. I told her there was no one better than me. "Ms. Smith," I said repeatedly. "With your help I will win." I knew I had to pull this off. Ms. Smith finally said, yes. I had convinced her. My mother was so proud of me. Mom went out and bought me a crown. I thought she was going a little over board. I had originally wanted three different patterns mixed into one. Ms. Smith said, "Doris that is too much, and the pattern would be too hard to make." I told her she could make the pattern. She would not let me do that. I told her I had to make sure I won. The one pattern I chose was a Vogue pattern, which was one of the hardest patterns. Vogue is a better- looking, finished product. Ms. Smith kept on saying we'd better win. We have to keep up our image. I kept telling her with her help I would win. I was so determined and focused! My mother got me all the material, the underlining, the seam binding, the interfacing, the thread and anything else that I needed to make my dress. I could not let down the girls before me who won.

My dress was metallic gold, high busted with gold trim around the armholes. As the dress came down it flared out like a trumpet. I put gold trim around the bottom of the dress. The dress was underlined with a thin material. Then it had a slick gold lining, and I had seam binding on each seam on the inside. All seams had seam binding. In addition, I made a long cape to the floor. The cape did not have any armholes. It just went around and fastened under the neck. I had that trimmed in white ostrich feathers, all around the whole cape. When I got finished with the dress, it was so beautiful! I was so proud of myself and with my clothing teacher, Ms. Smith. I told her "Thank you for believing in me because without your help, I could have never done that well on my prom dress." She instructed me all the way on my dress. My mother kept a picture of me on her mantel me back stage with the envelope in my hand and tears running down my face.

When I did something wrong, Ms. Smith would make me take it out and do it over repeatedly until I got it right. I did everything she told me to do because I knew she knew best. I had refused to be defeated. I got so tired of taking a loss over and over again until every seam was clean with no threads showing! The dress looked like it came from a high priced store. The dress was like something for a queen. This was a big accomplishment for my family and me. The day of the contest had finally arrived. All of the contestants had to turn in their garments a week before the contest, so the judges could examine each piece very closely. The judges already knew who the winner was. There were ten high schools in the contest, John Hay, John Adams, Jane Adams, East High, South High, Shaw, West Tech, East Tech, Glennville, and John. F. Kennedy. All the girls were back stage looking at each other's piece, admiring each other's work. All of our pieces were beautiful. I thought the girl from Jane Adams had a very good chance to win. She had made a suede black and beige pantsuit. She had the entire suit trimmed in rhinestones, but all the girls were saying I was going to win. I really felt in my heart that I had won; however, it could have been Jane Adams or me. She and I had the best pieces. It was time for the girls to put on our garments and walk onto the stage. It was very much like a fashion show. All ten of us were standing there on stage in front of all those people. I was so scared! I was standing there, shaking in my shoes. Mary Hope was the announcer. Each one of us was introduced and they said how each one of us worked so hard on our garments, but unfortunately, there was only one winner. The prize was a scholarship to a designer school. So now, the announcer called the five finalists and they were John. F. Kennedy (me), John Adams, Jane Adams, East Tech, and John Hay. Everyone else had to leave the stage. It was time to call the runner up. Before they did this, each of us had to take another walk down the runway. Here I was with this crown on my head and this long gown dragging on the floor. I was really feeling like a queen for a day. My entire family and my boyfriend, Fox, were there. Everyone clapped for us as we took our last walk down the runway. Boy! That was a day to remember! No matter who was the winner, it was a lot of fun. All the time, I am saying, "I've got to win. I've got to!" Then it was time for the runner-up to be announced. It was John Hay in fifth place, East Tech in fourth place, and John Adams in third place. Man-o-man, my heart was beating so fast! I was shaking so hard that one could see that I was shaking. Now, it was only Jane Adams and John F. Kennedy. I said to myself, "Here we go again. I got this. *Please Lord, Please Let me Win!*" She and I were standing there looking at each other, holding hands, wishing each other the very best luck. They called the second runner up, it was Jane Adams. My heart stopped, "Oh my Lord! I have won!" *I have won! I was the winner.* I did not know what to do. I was frozen. I stood there in shock. The tears started running down my face. A camera was flashing in my face, and they brought me out a big bouquet of red roses and a white envelope. I had won a full scholarship to a designer school. I never used it because I could not draw and fear got in the way. It was so much fear within me. I was told to walk down the runway one last time. As I was walking, music was playing "Here She Comes, Miss

America." I was walking and crying. They were happy tears. I finally had done something right. Everybody was so proud of me. The narrator was also one of the judges. She said, "Doris is the winner from John F. Kennedy High School, and a very fine job she has done. "She started telling the audience exactly what I had underneath my dress and all the hand stitches that were done. The dress took me a long time, and I put a lot of hard work into it. I had been a winner all the time, and I just did not know it. It was all worth it in the end. She made a wise crack about my outfit, and asked "Is it mink or what?" I had to take another walk down the runway; I had my bouquet of red roses in my arm along with my envelope. I could not wipe my tears because my hand was full. The cameras were steadily flashing, a whole lot of flashing. We went back stage, and my family and others met me, still congratulating me taking more pictures. There were so many people backstage! I thought I was famous or something. Everybody wanted to kiss me all over. I saw my mother. I went to her and she asked me why I was crying. I said what I used to say all the time, I answered I did not know, knowing I am a big baby and I never liked a lot of attention. My mother asked me again why I was crying. I said I finally succeeded in something. My mother was angry as a young girl as well. Mom told me about how she made homemade quilts. The principal of the school put her on Front Street showing off her work and Mom got embarrassed. The principal bought the quit. I was very, very, happy that I won first place. I made Ms. Smith happy. I was the first junior to enter the contest and I won. That was very special to me.

When I got back in school that Monday, everybody was congratulating me again. On the main floor of our high school in the showcase, my name appeared on a plate, along with the basketball players. I was so pleased and proud of myself. Just like today, I am very proud of my accomplishments. I did this without anyone cheating, without anyone picking a favorite. I won because my garment was the best. I always wanted to be the best at whatever I did. Now, at the age of 60, all my hard work and accomplishments were being praised. My church members saw it in me when I was a young adult. I am a leader. The sewing class gave me a party. All the girls who had won from

Kennedy before me were there, and my sewing class. Honoring me, I felt really big and important, even if it was only for a weekend. I earned it and it had paid off.

Then it was back to normal days. All the excitement was over. Ms. Smith was still prodding me about wanting to stay in the sewing room all day. But, Ms. Smith was very proud. She could not show any favoritism, and I understood that. She really was like a second mother to me. As the school continued, everything got back to normal.

I started having trouble with one girl, Marcie. She liked my boyfriend. He used her to get gifts for me. I guess her family had money. She got what she wanted from him, a baby. He loved me and she knew it. One time, I was in class. My girlfriend, Shelia, came to get me out of class. She said, "Jean, Marcie is downstairs in the bathroom talking about Fox being her man, and she was writing Marcie and Fox all over the walls." Shelia and I entered the bathroom. There was Marcie standing in front of the mirror with four of her friends. They all knew he was having sex with her. I had only Shelia with me, but I still was not scared of them. I walked up to her and said, "What's up with this?" As I looked around the bathroom walls, Shelia was right. It was everywhere, "Marcie and Fox." I started laughing. She said, "I don't know what you are laughing for because it is true. I said, "He could never pick you over me." I asked her how long their relationship had been going on. She said, "A long time, right under your nose and you did not know anything about it." I said, "Well, I'm happy for you because if you got Fox, that means I never had him in the beginning." She got angry and I made her angrier. I said, "If he is your man like you say why is it that you all are never around each other? He has never taken you anywhere other than to bed." I laughed and began to walk out of the bathroom. My girlfriend wanted me to fight her because of the way she was disrespecting me. I said, "No! I am better than that. I know what is up, and she does too. I am not going to fight her over any man, especially mine." So we left. I told Shelia that she was going to do something else to me to make me fight, watch and see.

As the school year continued, Christmas and my birthday were coming up. Fox asked me what I wanted. I told him a black, long, leather coat. He got it for me. In January of that year, we went back to school and I waited for a while to wear my coat to school. I did not want to keep my coat in my locker. Someone just might have gotten the idea to take my coat. After all, people were breaking into students' lockers. I had asked Ms. Smith, my sewing teacher, if she would keep my coat in her locker. She said, "Yes." One-day word had gotten to me that Marcie was trying to get my coat from Ms. Smith. I went to get my coat, and Ms. Smith said, "Doris, some little girl came and tried to get your coat. She said you told her to come and get your coat." I said, ok, Ms. Smith, *"I will see you later."* I walked away very fast. Ms. Smith said, "Doris, what are you going to do?" I did not answer her. I just kept on walking. Ms. Smith knew I had never sent anyone to get my coat, not even my best friend. I did not want to start other people pick up my coat because if someone wrong went to get my coat, such as Marcie, Ms. Smith might have given it to her.

I went to find Shelia. I was very upset, knowing that Marcie was trying to steal my coat., "I told Shelia I was going to beat her up. If none of her people jump on me, then she don't jump in either." I said. I found her at her favorite spot, which was in the bathroom, getting high.

I told Marcie that she was dumb, and that she was paying my man Fox. I also told her I did not have to pay Fox for anything. "So you just keep the money coming to him," I said. That was enough talk for me, because I said what I had to say to her, and she was going to keep running off at her mouth. I hit her right in her mouth. I was taking my coat off, beating her at the same time. I had given my coat to Shelia. No one jumped in, and as usual, she was beat up. I guess Marcie did not mind the ass beating. I was tired of her messing with me because of my boyfriend, somebody she would never get. However, she did have his baby. I was out of school for a week, and she went to the hospital. She never came back to school. I understand she got pregnant. She never graduated either.

The word had gotten out that her three or four sisters were looking for me. That was fine with me. I did not know her sisters, and I did not know what they were capable of doing to me. I was scared, but they never knew it. There was a dance hall where we used to go to all the time after school, mostly every day. It was an old bowling alley, not too far from my house. Back then, I was good for wearing wigs myself. I had gotten this idea from Foxy Brown's movies. I put razor blades all in my wigs, so when a girl put her hands in my hair to pull it, like most girls did when they fought, she would get cut. I never had any fingernails. I had a pop bottle top from a 16-ounce pop bottle. The pop bottle had rough edges. I had two of those put in between my index and middle finger. It made a nice weapon to scratch their face. I did this for about a week and never saw the sisters. Then all of a sudden, there they were. They appeared from nowhere. There were two of them. Fox and I were at the dance after school. I stayed in the bathroom to talk to both of Marcie's sisters, to let them know how their sister had been messing with me. I walked out the bathroom fast to go back to the dance to get Fox. I told him they were in the bathroom. He told them both that if they were thinking about jumping on me, that would get him into it. Therefore, nothing happened because I did not think they wanted any part of the two of us.

Marcie and I both stayed involved with Fox at first. Wow, I thought, I am in the 12th grade, a senior! I never thought I would have made it. At the time, it seemed as though I had been in school all my life. The 12th grade was really something different, the fact that I was a senior and about to graduate. The senior class always did different things. Homecoming was coming up. We had a picnic, parties, and various other activities. My boyfriend, dropped out of school after the 11th grade. I tried to get him to continue school. He had only a year left to finish, but he said he could not. He just did not like school. He still was always up at the school during recreation periods to watch me and to dance. He was a bad influence on me because I started cutting school really badly to be with him. If it were not for my girlfriend, Shelia, who talked me into taking an art class with her, I would not have graduated. I would not have had enough credits. I messed around and failed a class, but that art class gave me just enough credits to graduate with my class.

Shelia and I

CHAPTER THREE

Being Molested Again

I thank God for the class of 1973. I can say that one thing about all of my brothers and sisters. My parents with no education made sure all six of their chidden graduated from high school, and that is a blessing. After the school year got started really well, it seemed like the seniors were running everything. I did not stay in school a lot of times because my boyfriend had me cutting all the time with him. As I look back on the situation, Fox did not care if I graduated or not. I was in a program called co-op whereby I went to school a half a day and worked the other half of the day. Now that was up my alley because I loved to dress and I loved money. My parents could not afford to buy what I wanted, so I worked for it and bought my own clothes. I had been working since the age of 13. I got my first job with the summer program in school. I got my first car when I was in the 11th grade. It was not a new car but was something for me to get around in, and I was proud of it. A decent car took me where I wanted to go. I was proud to drive my girlfriends and myself to the basketball games, football games, and track meets. I never missed games because there was too much excitement at the games. There was this one young man on the basketball team named

Bobby Franklin who I had a crush on, but he never knew it. I used to love just looking at his body and watching him play ball.

Prom was coming. I had been ready for that year when I was in the 11th grade. The only things I needed were shoes, stockings, gloves and probably a purse. At the prom, the food was really good. We also took pictures, danced, and had fun. The after prom party was the "Bomb." Just about, everybody was getting high off weed, and we were drinking as well. At the end of the night, it was time for us to get a room. I did not get permission from my parents to stay out all night. It was prom night and that only came once in a lifetime. I did call her just to tell her that we were staying out a little later so she would not be worried. Four of us got the room together. My best girlfriend Shelia and her man Poochie, my man Fox and I. Poochie and Fox were best friends. I really did not like the idea because we did not have any kind of privacy. We could not afford to get a room to ourselves. All four of us had sex quietly, so one couple could not hear the other. We could not let our hair down and make love like we wanted to. The next morning we woke up, took a shower, got dressed and left the hotel to go home, and then changed to get ready for the picnic. When I got home, my parents did not say much to me. My mother just asked me if I had fun and how everything was and where we were on our way to next. I talked to her for a while, explaining our day that we had planned. We got to the picnic and it was nice. We had fun there as well. It was way out, taking us 45 minutes to get there. Once we arrived, there were a lot of people that were already there. Some of the guys were barbecuing, and some people were playing volleyball. Others where down at the beach. Some were out in the parking lot hanging out. I was one of those who had a hangover.

I really could not enjoy myself too much because I was sick. I was trying to rid of that hangover that I had. Some of the people said to take another drink, and then I would feel better. I was taking Alka-Seltzer and some of everything else. It seemed like nothing helped. I sat in the car a while. When the food got ready, I ate and felt a little better. By the time the picnic was over, later on that evening, I felt much better, and I was ready to party again. Everybody else was dead tired. Everyone went home to get some rest. School was still in session for another week before our commencement. The seniors really did not have to do anything much the last week of school but take our final exams. The seniors were really practicing for our big day, the commencement. We practiced how to walk, where to sit, and how to walk on stage. We had to practice the songs we were going to sing as a senior class and those who had solos. We did the "Star Spangled Banner." Now it was the night of commencement. This was one of the happiest days of my life. As we marched down the aisle, we formed the letters J.F.K. for John. F. Kennedy. Everyone had said how pretty our letters were. The people were clapping when we came out and marched to our seats. The ceremony seemed like it took forever. They had to talk and talk. It took forever to pass out the diplomas. Once the ceremony got started, we had a few class clowns. This one guy walked across the stage after he got his diploma in his hand. He pulled out this flat thing and popped it out. It was a tall hat and he put it on his head. It was so funny that everyone laughed. Then there was this other guy who, after getting his diploma, broke out with some shaving cream and put it on his face a little, then he had a razor. He started shaving. I know it was a good feeling that came over him. I know that I felt good that I had made it. Neither of the class clowns rehearsed those routines with us. We were young adults now. It was very humongous because what could anyone do? Nothing, it was a very hard struggle that last year. We all made it, at least most of us did. After commencement, everyone went to the basement to take pictures with our friends and families. The senior class of John F. Kennedy also had our last party. This would be the last time we would see each other because some students went on to college, the service, jail, some moved out of state, others got killed and some turned to drugs. I was not ready to leave high school, and I did not know what I wanted to do or become in life at the time. I just wanted to continue to have fun. I guess I thought I was going to stay young and fine as wind all of my life.

After high school, I kept working in the woman Bouquet where I was working while in high school. My scholarship that I had won from the high school competition was to a designer school. I did not use it, and I lost it. I could not draw. I just love to sew, and I thought that I could not learn how to draw. At first, I wanted to be a sewing teacher until I found out all of the classes that were required, such as chemistry for one. That one class totally discouraged me from becoming a teacher. I was always scared. The scholarship went down the drain because I was too fearful to use it. I got tired of the same old thing, still working as a sales girl at the boutique.

I decided to go to school at Cuyahoga Community College, Metro campus Downtown Cleveland. I got there and found it was like a high school with students from all over going there. I had missed all the fun we had in high school. I did not know how to change and grow up. I did not learn too much because at the time, I really did not want to do anything. I had a grant to attend college. The refund monies were good. After all classes, tuition, and books were paid for and there would be a big refund check issued. The money was good. Every three months I got around three hundred dollars. Today, I know that was not a lot of money. Back then, I thought it was. That refund money was the only thing that kept me in school. I was making grades like Cs and Ds, and I did not care. I stayed in school for a year, and out for two years, and then I got a job at Richmond Brothers doing piecework on a power sewing machine. The pay was good. I took home between three and four hundred dollars a week depending on how hard I worked. I stayed at Richmond Brothers for almost two years until one day we had this big sale. We made men's clothes, mostly suits. At the sale, there was just about everything there: Men's suits, sweaters, jackets, leather items, pants, shirts and various other items. Items were 50% off. The store was not opened to the public. I got my man friend some clothes. I was one of the faster piece workers there. Here I go losing another job. "Now, I am out of a job again. What am I going to do?" I was living by myself; had no children, but I had many bills. Nevertheless, the first thing I did was to sign up for unemployment. It took so long before I started receiving any money. I also applied for welfare. Welfare for me was at that time general relief because I had no children. I was getting $147.00 a month and $100.00 in food stamps. The food stamps were OK but the money would not even pay my rent. I had to sell some of my stamps, and I still did not have enough to make ends meet. I started messing around with different men, getting money. I got tired of that fast. I never liked being told what to do and for a man to crowd me, that was out of the question. I did not like taking orders from anybody. I started stealing clothes and cashing checks that I had stolen. You name it; I was doing it. I was doing things to make money that I had no business doing because I really was not the type. I was trying to be in the "In crowd" which cost me very dearly. I was not on drugs at the time; I did not care about any consequences. I kept on stealing and getting caught time after time again. I kept on catching case after case. I got put onto probation time and time again until I got tired and said to myself, "Something has to change". I was still with my boyfriend Fox, and I went ahead and moved in together, and all hell broke out. He was sneaking around still seeing his baby's mother, Marcie, which he thought I did not know about. I was hearing all kinds of things such as he was letting her drive my car because at the time he did not have one. When I confronted him with the problem, he and I started fighting. He totally denied everything. He had the nerve to ask me if he could bring his baby, Robert Jr. to our house. I told him "Hell no". I did not want that child around me, because I did not want to take my anger out on the baby because he did not ask to be born, and he did not know the hell I had gone through with his mother. I might have wanted to kill the baby or do something stupid because I disliked his mother so much. Fox cheated on me to bring that child into the world. I could not accept that or his son. Shortly after all of that had taken place, Fox and I had got on bad terms with each other, and I wanted him to leave my house. He told me that he was not going anywhere and that it was his apartment as well. I could not take any more of his bullshit. I moved back home with my mother for a while and let him keep the apartment.

After all that had happened to me, I decided that I needed a job, a good job. I looked up, and I had gotten myself hired at Concord Manor Nursing Home as the junior accountant. The place was Black owned. I went for an interview; Mr. Green took a liking to me because of the way I talked, and what I had to say about the job, and the way I came across to him was very impressive. Mr. Green told me he liked the drive I had about the job and myself. I told him in the interview that I was the woman for the job, and I could do it if I was given the chance. Mr.

Green gave me that job, and he gave me the chance to prove myself. I did not let him down at first. He was very proud of the way I grasped onto the job duties and noticed the material so quickly. The woman who trained me was very nice. She had a lot of patience, Ms. Smith was her name, and she was a very knowledgeable woman about the business. She had been offered a better position. She trained me very well; I wanted to learn everything I possible could that would only make me a better asset to the company and a very knowledgeable person about his business. Ms. Smith stayed with me for a month until I felt comfortable about going on my own. I had to go to the bank twice a week to make deposits. I did all the journal entries, trial balances, debits and credits. I even wrote out the checks for payment to different companies for bills, but the boss had to sign them. The job went very well until after about a year, I got a little crazy and wanted to dip into the "Cookie jar". I started writing my own checks out for myself, signing my boss's signature; I was going to the bank, cashing checks in a friend's name. He had no idea it was I until he came to the jail to identify me. Mr. Green was really hurt because he had trusted me. The police let Mr. Green talk to me. I had been in jail for two days before he saw me. He said, "Doris, I have never seen you look so bad. You are much too pretty of a young woman to be in here and to do the things you did. If you needed extra money for something, I would have given it to you. All you would have had to do was ask." I was so hurt and ashamed that I could not even look him in the eyes. I really thought I was being slick, but being slick does not pay, and I was only being slick to myself. I had a very good boss, he used to help me when my car broke down. He wanted to make sure I could go back and forth to work with no problems. He could have pressed charges against me. I had to repay the money over time. I got out of jail on bond. He told me if I ever needed someone to talk to, I knew where to find him. He also said that he hoped and prayed that I get my life together because I really was a good person. I had many past problems by life experiences. So many times, I wanted to talk to Mr. Green to apologize for what I had done to him, but I just could not bring myself around to doing that. I guess I had the devil in me, and I was very stubborn. I was out of a job again. Today he is dead as well.

I had decided to go back to school again. I was interested in accounting, so I went to Dyke College and made my major accounting. I was very active at Dyke. I had cheerleader tryouts. My girlfriend, Pat, bugged the mess out of me to try out with her; I really did not want to, but she talked me into it. I was so surprised when we both made the team. After the results, I was glad she had talked me into trying out for the team. I had to work with Pat because I could do the routines a little better than her. We would work very hard on our flips; round offs, and jumps as well as our splits.

Jean in the back with the short hair

I felt cheated because they would not let me make the team in high school. Better things came for me in college. The cheerleaders got to travel with the team on the bus to out of town games. Others times we had to get our own transportation for in town games and follow the bus. Sometimes at tournaments, us cheerleaders had a room for the weekend. All of the cheerleaders were in one room. We were clowning around, having fun, and taking pictures, on the bus in our room with the guy's and our coach. We sneaked into the basketball players' room, and they had wet underwear in the bathroom dripping wet. Their uniforms were all over the room, which was a turn off to us girls. We laughed at them so hard. We all had been drinking. The men's were not supposed to have drunk anything, but they did. Everything the guy's said to us, we laughed. Then there was a knock at the door; it was the coach checking on his players. The girls were on the boys bed' jumping up and down. We jumped off the bed and ran right passed the coach, laughing. Mr. Harris asked, "What the hell is going on in here?" He told our cheerleader representative that we were in the boys' room. Her name was Mrs. Jones, and she got on us about the situation. She told us that we had no business in the guy's room. We knew that. We told her we were just visiting. After all, most of us were in our twenties, and we wanted to be treated like young adults. Ms. Jones did state that was against the rules of Coach Harris. The next day was Saturday. It was the tournament. The guy's had three games to play. Whichever team won the best out of the three games would go on to play the big championship. That Sunday we won the two games out of three. It was Dyke College against Wooster College. It was a tie game; we went into overtime. In overtime we won by a basket. Dyke College was the Champs. The fans started going crazy. Many students had driven down to support the team. Afterwards, everyone got dressed and went out to dinner to celebrate. It was the Coach treat. After dinner, it was time to get on the road to head back to Cleveland. The team received a very big old trophy for the school showcase, and a small one for each player. All of the students were clowning on the bus the entire way back by singing songs, hanging out of the windows with our pom-poms until we left the schools grounds. It was a lot of fun. After a while, winter came, and it was something to look forward of. I made it through another quarter. School was out for the winter break. When we got back to school, the first of the year, I was a Year older. I knew my boyfriend really loved me, but we were young and it was time for me to move on and find me someone else.

One day my girlfriend, Martha said, "Doris, I know this guy that would love to meet you. I think you and Avery would make a good couple." I asked her what he looked like. She said he was about 6 feet tall, had light brown skin, built very nicely, and his hair was cut very close to his head. She continued, "I am sure you want to meet him," so I said, "OK!" I love tall men and I had nothing to lose.

Avery on your right with his cousin and me.

For my twenty- first birthday, Avery gave me a surprise birthday party, and indeed, it was a surprise. He set the whole thing up himself. I was surprised on how it pulled that off without me knowing about the party. Everybody was there. There was so much to drink and eat. I had the big party glass, and money was all over me. By it being in December, I was dressed nicely. He told me that we were going to a cabaret party. I had on this red metallic dress with no sleeves, and it fit my body. At the time, I was wearing about a size ten dress. I have always been very sharp with big hips, a small waist, and a big backside. I had on red shoes with a black, one-inch strap going across the front of the shoe. My hair was up with a red banana clip holding it up in place, red and black earrings and my white rabbit coat to top everything off. I was cleaner than clean. I looked very lovely. I stepped into the hall, and it did not look like a cabaret party. Just as I was about to ask him what this was, everybody came out of the wood- work and said 'Surprise." My mouth dropped open. I grabbed my face in surprise and started smiling from ear to ear. I looked at him and smiled, then gave him a big kiss and a hug. I was so happy! No one had ever given me anything like that before in my life. I was trying to really move away from Fox.

I was looking for a place to move to. I found an apartment down the street from my mother moved into an empty apartment; I had nothing but my clothes. I had a peace of mind away from Fox. I always had kept a job and I knew in time I would get on my feet. Avery and I hit it off really well, and I said to myself, "Oh-boy, here I go again." I was scared to get involved with Avery because Fox was so crazy. Avery ensured me that Fox was not going to do anything to me as long as he was around. Avery said he really liked me and that no ex-boyfriend was going to run him away. He was a very warm- hearted person. My mom loved Avery. I never liked to see two men get into it over me.

Avery went out and helped me pick out all new furniture, first a white bedroom set, then a navy blue print living room set, and a little kitchen table with chairs. He got a little at a time. He did not want to see me without; furthermore, he wanted to help me stay away from Fox for good. Avery was a real man to me because he did not want me to move in with him or he move in with me. He had a very nice apartment of his own. I told Avery everything about Fox because he once told me if he could not have me, no one could. I could not leave Avery blind about that situation. I told Avery that Fox was crazy. He said he was crazier. Fox found out where I lived. He used to always terrorize me. He watched me walk to the store and pulled a gun on me, telling me to get into his car, and then he would take me to his house to rape me. As long as I was with someone, he would not mess with me. As soon as he caught me alone, all the trouble started. He would kick in the door to my house. He broke my windows out. My property owner and I got tired of Fox's behavior I got tired of him mentally hurting me. I told Avery how Fox was harassing me. Then Avery started staying at my house a lot to get Fox from me.

Avery carried a gun. One evening the girl across the hall asked me for a cup of sugar. I said, "Sure, when you get ready for it, come on over." She replied, OK I told her that the door would be open. About 15 minutes after that, there was a knock at the door, I thought it was the girl across the hall, so I said, "Come on in," but it was Fox. I got up, ran to the door and asked him to leave, he looked at Avery then me, and Avery looked at him. Avery had his gun sitting on the table next to him. Fox saw the gun; he pushed me out the way. Avery never moved out of his seat. Fox walked over to Avery, they were still looking at each other, fox was so stupid, he tried to pick the gun up off of the table, but Avery was waiting for him to make a move like that. Avery was on top of the entire situation, he let Fox get almost to the gun then he grabbed it up, cocked it with quickness and told Fox not to take another step. The gun was pointed at his head. I said "Oh God, do not shoot him." I was so scared; I was scared for Fox because I knew if he had taken another step, Avery would have shot him. Fox turned around and left, he went to the telephone booth called me and said who was that nigger that pulled the gun on him. I told him that was my new man who was going to hurt him for messing with me, if he did not leave me alone. "He will be here every night with me." I even told Fox Avery's name because he asked me to. One day, as I was walking to the store Fox jumped out of a car and pulled a knife on me. He told me to get into the car. I did, he took me to his house and raped me again. Then he let me go. I did not understand why he was taking advantage of my body like that, but once was not enough for him. He did that same thing three times to me. The third time, I went straight to the police station with his semen still inside of me. I had all the proof of rape. Later that night two detectives came to talk to me. They asked me if I knew the man. I told them, "Yes," he was my ex-boyfriend who would not leave me alone. They asked me if I was sure that I wanted to press charges. I said, "Yes," he leaves me no choice. Fox could not just keep taking my body when he felt like it. He could not just keep trying to destroy my life with other men who want to talk to me. The detective told me that I should not have made it so good for him. I smiled and said, "Well, we had been together seven years." The report was taken. Now, Fox had a rape charge on his record. The detective also told me that there would be a warrant out for his arrest that made me feel a little better. A week later Fox came back to get me again, but by this time Avery had given me a gun so that Fox would not rape me again, and he did not. As soon as I saw Fox, I pulled the gun on him and I said, "If you put your hands on me or take another step towards me, I will have to shoot you." The gun was shaking in my hand. He did not dare take another step because he knew I was scared and crazy enough to shoot his ass. When a person is scared, there is no telling what he or she might do. Now, Fox wanted to talk. I told him that it was too late for that. I did not want to talk to him. I told him just to leave me alone. I told him that I had put a rape charge on him which I should not have told him. He said, "What?" I said, "Oh, you are going to leave me alone one way or the other."

I also told him, "As soon as the police catch you, you will be in jail." I told him that was his entire fault, not mine. I walked away from him, and he kept saying that he did not believe this shit. I said, "I could not believe you were pulling a knife on me to get me to do what you wanted me to do."

It took the police over five years to catch Fox. They told me if I ever see him, I could call and they would pick him up. He had moved to a different address and no one was telling me where he was. Then one night my girlfriend and I were out dancing at the Forge Night Club. I spotted his truck, so I went back inside and told one of his friends that I was going to call the police on him. His friend said, "Jean, don't do that." I said, "His ass never cared about me, so why should I give him a break?" I went and made the call. His friend went and called him and told him that I had called the police. When they got there and stopped the truck, Fox was not driving it. The police had told me to stay right there where I was, and I did that. They decided to check *me* out. I did not have anything to hide; I knew my record was clean. I gave then my license as they asked me to do. They ran a check on me, and founds out that there was a warrant out for me. I said, "There is no way, for what?" I asked. The police said, "Robbery." I said, "I never robbed anybody in my life. Whom was I supposed to have robbed?" They said "A man named Robert Fox." They had to take me in. I was so embarrassed. I was as clean as a whistle, and all of my friends were standing outside alone with other people who I did not know. The police put me into the car and drove off. Once I got to the station, I found out that Avery and I had supposedly robbed Fox. He had made a report the week after he found out that I had a rape charge on him. Thank God, Avery was a very honest man with no criminal record. He had never been in any kind of trouble. I told the police my side of the story. Fox my ex-man kept on raping me so I put a rape charge on him. He got very angry about that. I called Avery that night and told him what was going on. I had to spend the night in jail because there was nothing he could have done that night. I did not like that too much, but I had no choice in the matter. Avery told me that he would be there to get me out the first thing in the morning. Avery's story and my story checked out to be true. The police let me go with no charges. Avery was very upset because Fox told a lie on the both of us. Avery said he knew where to catch him. Avery started hanging out at the Forge Night Club where all of us used to go without telling me. Avery had never gone there because he said that place was just not his style. He really was not a dancer. He wanted to catch Fox to confront him about lying on us. Avery finally saw Fox, he said he walked up to him and said, "Hey man," "Don't they call you Fox?" Fox said, "No," "You sure as hell look just like that nigger named Fox". He then said, "Man, I told you my name is not Fox." See, Fox could fight me, but when it came time for him to fight a man, he could not do that. Avery knew all the time he was talking to Fox. Why did Fox lie about who he was? I think because Fox knew he could not fight, and Avery would have "warmed his ass."

Avery came back home and told me that Fox denied who he was. We laughed so hard. They knew who each one was from seeing each other at my house that time when Avery had pulled his gun on him. Fox was trying to play Avery for a big fool. Avery wanted to move me from that apartment, and get me another one, but I refused to let Fox run me away from my pace of residence. Avery said that just to keep confusion down, it would be better for me to move. I stayed there for another year. Meanwhile, Fox slowly left me alone because the police were looking for him.

Avery had come out of the clear blue sky with some new news for me that I had no knowledge of. He said his ex-wife was about to have his baby. I said, "What?" He had not told me. He had told me that he was going through a divorce, but he never told me she was pregnant with his child. As he was telling me the news, I had spent the night at his house; I had on one of his big shirts, no bra and no underwear. I was in the kitchen cooking us some breakfast when he told me the bad news. I never got breakfast finished. That was just how bad he hurt me. I asked him, "Why did you not tell me, and why did you wait so long.?" We had been talking for almost six months. He told me because he really did like me a lot and he did not want to chase me away with that news. I told him that I liked him just that much and that maybe that news would not have made a difference if he had told me up front. He should have left that decision up to me. It was not fair how Avery handled that situation. I tried to understand, but he was just not true to me. We started having problems because he was the kind of man who was going to do the right thing by his family. He told me that he had agreed to let his ex-wife move back in with him until the baby got to be a few months old and she got back on her feet. She was still in love with him and I knew that. She was using the baby as an excuse to get him back, so she thought. He told me nothing was going to change between him and me and that everything would still be the same. After she had the baby, she did move in with him. She and the baby had their own separate bedroom, and Avery did not have anything to do with her sexually, so he said. I could not call him any more at his house because he wanted to give her all the respect in the world. I asked him that "If you did not have anything to do with her other than helping her out with the baby and I am your women, then why I cannot call you at home? He said, "Just because." I said, "Just bullshit." I reinforced to him that he had said nothing was going to change. That was a lie. I felt that he did not want her to know about me. I had to get in touch with him at his job, or he would come by to check on me just about every night after he got off work. He would not stay that long as if he had to hurry up and get home to her. I did not like that. I got very tired of being second. However, he did not see me as being second because he was a man, or he did see it and he just did not want to admit the truth. I understood him wanting to do the right thing by his child, but I was not going to continue to let him hurt me and neglect my wants and wishes. As time went on, I got tired of him sneaking over to my house and rushing to leave. He would leave me money, but our relationship was not the same.

I had gotten a new job that was in telephone sales for home improvements. I did a nice job at selling; it was a part-time job. I met a man I worked with, his name was Reggie Sims, and we were very good friends; we were cool with one another. He took time with me, and he made me feel as though I was wanted. Avery used to make me feel like that all the time. My new friend was one of the top sales representatives the company had. He taught me a lot about our job. He helped me to sale more, where I made more money. We also went to the horse track a lot, and he was good on how to pick the horses as well. I really did not care too much for the horses.

I told Avery I was seeing someone else. He said, "Why Jean, why you cannot wait? It is only a short time." I told him that he does not spend time with me anymore, we did not do anything anymore, and I just could not stand to continue waiting around for him to make up his mind about his ex-wife and his baby. I did not like the fact that he thought he could put my life on hold. I did not think that was fair to me, but all he cared about was himself and his family and not me. I told him that I still was in love with him, and if he wanted me to wait on him, I would rather wait on him with somebody. He had somebody, but he did not want me to have anyone. I got tired of understanding. I had also told him that I would continue to see him.

Ron, Gwen, and I

Eventuality as time passed Reggie and I were having problems because he was going through a divorce. I said to myself, "What is it that I keep getting these men who are going through a divorce." He wanted to live together, but I just could not do that because he had two small children who I did not want to get involved with that situation. I went ahead and lived with him, Avery and I had broken up.

Two months later Avery got in touch with me and said that he kept his word to me. His wife was gone. I told him I did not believe him. He was just trying to get me back because he thought he had lost me for good. It was true; I was out done. Sometimes it pays to be still. I was not in love with Reggie; I always thought Avery was a better man, he said he and I would always be friends until the day he died, and we were friends, and he always stayed in touch with my family. We even had tried to get back together from time-to-time, but things were never the same. Sometimes it pays to be still. After a year with Reggie I got tired of him and his children and I left him. This is when Avery and I got back together, but he wanted to have other women as well, and I was not going for that.

Then, there I went again looking for a job, back to Mom's house again. I found myself a job at the bank as a teller. At the time, I did not know if a person who had a record could work at the bank or not. I had never been to prison, but I did have a felony record at the time. I was just that foolish. They took my fingerprints. When I asked what they were taking them for, they said the prints were going to Washington, D.C. to see if any records I had would come back on me. I got scared. At the time, it took about six months for the prints to come back. I said to myself, "If I get the bank teller employment and do a good job, when my prints come back, they might still keep me on. What I did not know was that the bank could not knowingly employ any person with a felony. Every time my boss said, "Doris, I need to see you, my heart dropped. I was the best teller. For some reason I had it in me to steal. I had never worked around so much money in all my life. Every day I wanted to take me a handful of money. I did not because I really was thinking about my job. I was gathering information whereby I could use it at a later date if need be. I was getting people's account numbers that had more than six thousand dollars in their accounts. I really thought I was doing something smart. All the time I was only hurting myself. The things that I did, I want you to know that I am not proud of any of it that is where my life lead me it was very bad behavior. God has changed me, and it was a very hard road and a very costly hard lesson. However, that is the life I choose and the path I went down at that time in my life. I kept a record of all the information that I needed to withdrawal money from people accounts at a later date if I was fired from that job for what every reason. I was caught and I paid dearly. All the money that I had taken, I paid that out in lawyers' fees and more, and then I still went to the penitentiary. My boss at the bank was getting ready to promote me to head teller. He had already told me I was supposed to start that following week. He always played around with the tellers in a humorous way. Before the end of the week, he said, "Doris, may I speak with you in my office?" I said, "Oh boy! What have I done now?" By this time, I had forgotten all about my fingerprints. I thought he wanted to talk with me about my promotion or something. He came with the bad news; I could not do anything but drop my head in shame. He said that there was nothing he could do. He told me it was nothing to be ashamed of. I had made a mistake, but unfortunately, the bank could not keep me on. He talked to me, I started crying. I told him all my life I had tried so hard, but society wound not let me do it fair and the right way. I had paid my dues; my boss was telling me that he was going to see if he could get me a job at this credit union. He knew the manager over their very well, and my boss was a very known and respected man. H said it would take some time. I waited and waited until I could not wait any longer. I guess things did not come fast enough for me, and I did not have any patience. I thought that all the information that I had gathered up previously from the bank was time for me to use. I had lost another job. At the time I could not understand why I kept losing job after job. To withdraw money, I went to the same kind of bank as I was working at and to one of the girls I had gone to teller school with. She had remembered me and was glad to see me. Although she did not remember my name, she remembered my face. I was not using my name; I knew she would not remember my name anyway. Where I messed up at is that I could not stop; the money got really good but I was like the most stupid criminal. I would not go back to the same bank; I found out where some of the other girls where that I had gone to teller school with were. I would take out between five and one thousand dollars from each bank. I do not remember how I got the money, but I did. I did this sometimes, two and three times a day. I did not get to use the money because it all went to a lawyer when I got caught. The last time I should have known better. I had become taking people for granted. This was the slowest girl in training school so I though. This female supervisor came over to her and asked if there was a problem.

She said, "No," and explained to her what I wanted to do. The girl told her supervisor that I had gone to teller school with her, and the woman was looking over her and saw the name on the withdrawal slip. Well, it was a white woman's name on the slip. She butted into our conversation and asked me for my ID. I got scared and felt uncomfortable. I told her it was in the car. What I did not know was that they had a police officer in the bank already in the back room unless they had two ways of getting into the bank. I did not think they did. It was a rainy day. My umbrella was on the floor. I picked it up, turned around, and headed for the door. The bank had double doors; I got in between the doors getting ready to push the door leading to the outside. All of a sudden, someone tapped me on the shoulder. I turned around, and it was the police, I said to myself "Oh shit." I said, "Yes, may I help you?" He said," I am sorry, Madam. May I speak with you?" I said to myself again, "Oh shit." I went back inside the bank and had a seat. I was very embarrassed because I had gotten caught. I had so much ID on me, all kind of stuff that did not belong to me. It was from all the banks that I had been to that day. At least I was smart enough to have taken the money home and hide it. I was grateful for that. After I sat down, the police officer showed me his badge, introduced himself to me, and said I did not have to talk to him if I did not want to. Being senseless and not knowing any better, I went ahead and talked to him a little. He asked me if I had any ID's that showed the real me. I also told him it was in the car. He asked me if he could look into my purse, I said, "No, for what?" I do not know what I was thinking—maybe he would let me go. Instead, he told me I was under arrest for investigation. I said, "For what?" He replied "Grand theft." I said, well, I do not have anything else to say. He hand cuffed me and took me downtown to book me. My car was towed; I should have told him someone had dropped me off. At the time, I was living with Reggie. Once I got to the police station I called him and told him that I was in jail. He was shocked. He had no idea of what I was doing because I did not tell him; me being in jail was a total surprise. I had to tell him where I had hidden my money in the house because he had to come and get me out of jail. When I told him how much money I had gotten, his mouth fell wide open. Crime does not pay. He could not understand how I had done all of that without him knowing. Just to show that people do not know people like they think they do sometimes. He had to get my car out of impound and me out of jail. I was charged with forgery, thief, and receiving stolen property. My bond was set at $2,500.00. It cost $280.00 to get out of jail. Once I was out, I had to look for a good lawyer. I had never been to the penitentiary yet, and I did not want to go. I kept on doing wrong; and no one could help me out of the trouble that I had gotten myself into. Lawyers could only do so much, especially when I kept doing the same thing repeatedly. I hired a lawyer who was supposed to be good. I would have the money to her before the day was out, and I did. She guaranteed me that I would not have to do any time. I told her that was what I was paying her for. I did not want to do a day. These charges happened in 1982. They had me running back and forth to court for the arraignment to change my Plea, and Pre-trail. It was all really scary, knowing the unknown.

I got so tired of running back and forth to court. I just wanted it all to be over. In the meantime, I was feeling funny about Reggie and I relationship; I had wanted to break up with him. I moved all of my things back to my mom's house because I felt that I could not trust him anyone. Reggie kept on telling me I did not have to do that. I started not believing in him. He had told me just in case things went wrong, he would keep my place and everything would be at my place when I got out. Something inside of me kept saying, "Do not trust him." I had said if anything did happen to me, I would of felt better if my mother had all my things. I put many of my things in storage. I told him I could not think of him having another woman lying in my bed and using my stuff. If he wanted to stay in an empty apartment, I did not have a problem with that. After I had cleaned out my apartment, he did not want to stay there. We were still seeing each other until the day I got sentenced. All the time he told me no matter what, he will be there for me, but I really did not trust him at all anymore. I had got in touch with my old friend Avery and told him what I had done, and the trouble I was in; he told me that was a very smart move I did to move back with my mother. I was not married to Reggie. Avery was right there for me, like he had said, "Friends until the end." He meant every word of that, and he did not have a problem proving it to me. I still trusted him, and I was still in love with him. I knew he cared a great deal for me. He always had and always will care about me. He was about the best man I have ever had. It was finally time for me to be sentenced. My lawyer took me in one of the back rooms across from the courtroom, after going into the judge's chambers. My lawyer said, "Doris, I am sorry. I think you have to do a little time." I could not believe what I was hearing, and I did not want to believe her. I kept on telling her that I do not want to do a day. "That is what I paid you for," I said. She kept telling me the same thing about doing time. My sentence was one to five years for forgery. Receiving stolen property was dropped. My sentence was run together, meaning concurrently. I said, "Oh shit, what have I gotten myself into now?" A friend told me to listen for the judge to say, "Sentence suspended." However, I never heard that; all I heard was one to five, one to five concurrent, transport as soon as possible (ASAP) to the Ohio Reformatory for Woman. I was still standing in front of the judge waiting for the judge, to say, "Sentence suspended," but she never said that. The deputy sheriff walked up to me with the handcuffs. I was looking all around to say, "What is going on?" What the judge had said still had not soaked into my mind that I was on my way to the penitentiary, The Big House. I busted out and said "Oh no, Your Honor, please do not send me to that place, I do not belong there." The judge looked at me; she then got up and walked away. I was in this room right outside the courtroom; they took the handcuffs off me, and then walked away. I did not know what was going on. After sitting alone for a while, a woman deputy came and said, "Come with me?" She said well, "We are going to book you in, and you will stay in the county for a week or two. That way your family and friends can come see you before it's time." I said, "Time for what." I said, "What is going to happen is you will ride off to Marysville." I told my mother I was not coming back home. Mom said, "Jean," Why are you saying that. In addition, I said, "Because the only thing I knew about prison is what I had seen on TV." I had never known anybody who had gone to prison to know what it was like. I had no one to give me a word of advice to tell me how it really was. I said, "There is no one that is going to take anything from me?" I meant that. I told Mom she might as well get ready to make my funeral arrangements because if they tried to jump me, one thing is for sure. I would get each one of them; therefore, those women would have to kill me. My mother told me not to go there getting into trouble. I really did not know what I was saying. I was scared of the un-known, but I meant every word I said at the time. I also told the woman officer that I do not think I will be going back home. The officer said, "Oh,' it is not that bad. You do not need to be talking like that." She told me that I probably would get shocked out after thirty days. Well that did not happen for me. I asked what shock was. She told me that my lawyer could file a motion for shock probation and the county would bring me back home. Then I would finish my time on probation. My lawyer never filed the paperwork because I still owed her money. My family knew that I stayed in trouble, true enough I stayed pretty much to myself,and I did not really have what you call friends; men were my friends which all they wanted was what was under my dress, my good stuff, and I was too stupid to really realize that. However, not all men were like that. I felt that a woman would stab me in the back as soon as I turned around; they are very conniving. I did not trust women at all. I was scared of them, and my mother used to tell me all the time that I could not live in this world by myself. I used to try by shutting everyone out of my life.

CHAPTER FOUR

Going to Marysville in Prison

One morning the guard woke me up along with four other inmates and said "Get your things together; it's time to ride out." The county never let anyone know when inmates are riding out because of security reasons. The fear of escape, or having someone sitting on the road ready to free the inmates, to me nothing like that would be worth it because then the inmate would have to be on the run, looking over his or her shoulder minute by minute, and that is no fun. I did not want to become a fugitive. We did not go straight to Marysville right away and that was good so I thought. We went outside of Columbus, Ohio to a big building that looked like a warehouse. I said, "Is this Marysville? They said, NO." This is what they called W.C.A.C, which meant admissions for new arrivals. It was supposed to get us ready for Marysville. Upon arriving there, it was told to me we would be in this W.C.A.C for six weeks. There were two sides. I was on the east wing which was for women just coming in to the facility. Each side was three weeks. When going to the west wing the next stop was the big house, Maryville called the farm and it is outside of Columbus, Ohio, as well.

WCAC was a living hell for me. There were three rows of fifty beds in each row. Toward the end of each row, there were five single beds. Those beds were for the older women or the ones who had medical problems. There were windows all over the place to enjoy the daylight because we could not go outside. I had a top bunk. There was a little cabinet to hang my nightgown and things like that. We also had to clean around our beds every morning on our hands and knees with kneepads on. We had to clean and mop the bathroom, showers, and the lunchroom. We cooked our own food with a supervisor. We also had to mop and keep our day room clean. It was all done on our hands and knees. I had never heard of anything so ridiculous in my life, and I hated it.

We had to get up in the mornings at 5 A.M. and had three minutes to wash up; everything was "hurry up" to do nothing. After washing up, we went back to make up our beds. Our beds had to be super tight like that saying goes a dime would pop off it. I thought I was in the army somewhere. After making the bed up, we had to sit on our beds until it was time for breakfast, which was at 5:45 A.M. More than one hundred woman had to wash up in minutes that routine was done every morning. After breakfast, we went into another room where we had to stay all day until it was time to go to bed, which was at 9:00 P.M. First, the east side would eat, and then the west side, but we all ended up in this big day room. We were like little children.

There were all kinds of games we could play during the day. There were cards, jacks, jump ropes, paddle and ball set's we also were allowed to do each other's hair. Everybody mostly wore braids. Some girls had perms. We even made purses out of newspaper. The correction officer C.O who was nothing but a baby sitter who was to watch us to make sure we followed the rules and did not get into trouble with each other. In addition, the C.O used to let us use the stapler to staple the sides of our homemade paper bag purse. We had all our little things in our purse such as paper, pens, and even food. Mostly everyone saved food because that was all we had gotten to eat. Sometimes we would have boiled eggs for breakfast. If we did not want to eat then, we would put the eggs into our purse and eat them later. I did not know at the time keeping food was "Contraband." It was our food! There was a shakedown one day, and our purses were searched from time to time. Some of us inmates had an egg in our purse. We got tickets for bad behavior. Our last meal of the day was at 5:00 PM. The tickets were heard once we got to Marysville. An inmate did not want to accumulate too many tickets because then she would be labeled a troublemaker. To me, W.C.A.C was a living hell. I said I am never coming back to this place. We could smoke, but we were not allowed to have matches or lighters. We could smoke every three hours for 15 minutes. The C.O. would call smoke break everyone would run up to her to get a light. She would light a few women cigarettes; the rest of the women got a light from each other. The room would be full of smoke because everyone was chain smoking, as many cigarettes as possible. When the C.O said, "Smoke break over, "everyone had to put out her cigarette. When a person is with criminals who think she is slick, it is expected for her, to find a way to do what is not expected of her to do. Some of the women had been at W.C.A.C. before or locked up before. There were ways to get a lighter into the place. In the evening when we went to the room to get ready for our showers and go to bed, the lighter got passed to get a few puffs from a cigarette. We had to be by a window or toward the back of the room so the C.O. could not see or smell the smoke. Like anything else, one always spoils it for the rest. One girl always got angry for one reason or another, or she fell out with the one that had the lighter. She would tell and get that person into trouble, and that is how it was. Usually it might take a while to get another lighter, but someone else would come in with a lighter or matches that she snuck in. It never failed; some body always told who had the lighter. After I saw how the women could not be trusted and that they would turn on you "With a drop of a dime," I did not want any part of that mess. It was a stupid game that the women were playing with their freedom. I did not really have any trouble, I stayed myself. I stood my ground. I was not into women, and I told them that. Seeing women kiss was nothing new for the C.O to see; however, it was against the rules. If the C.O. caught them, they would be in trouble. The women knew the rules, and they broke them anyway. All that stuff was rather new to me; I had never been around anything like that before. I used to look and say to myself, "What a shame." That is what I had eyes for, to look.

There were times when I just cried because I did not get much mail, and everybody was getting mail and cards and I was getting nothing. When I was in Admissions the first time, we could not call home. The few letters I did get were all bad news. My lawyer did not want to file my motion for "Shock probation," which would have meant I would have been home in 90 days. The lawyer demanded more money. She told my family to bring the title to my car. When mom told me the news, I really did not want to do that because I had lost faith in my lawyer and felt as if she was just going to take my money and do nothing for me to get me out of jail. Which I had no more money anyway. I had told my mother I would go ahead and sit the time out, not really knowing what I was saying. It was bad enough being locked up, but every time I got mail, my mother was talking about bills that I could not pay. I did not understand where she thought I was going to get money. I had my car paid for; it was not a new car but it was mine. I felt like my family hated me. My parents were from the South with no education; my mother had my sister or God-sister write the letters to me; that was embarrassing because that kept them in my business and I knew nothing about nobody else's business. Life was bad for me on a continually basis.

Everyone said I was one that got smart all the time; but I was 27 years old when I were sentenced on January 8, 1982

I had to pray a lot to ask God to keep me strong. My parents, grandparents, friends, and church members were praying for me a lot. I guess that is all they could do or wanted to do for me, especially my mother. I did not think my parents understood because neither one of them had ever been in jail or prison; I was just the black sheep in the family. My father cared for me more than my mother did because he had to make her do things for me. The other kids were not treated like that, especially my baby sister and my oldest sister. They could never do wrong in my mother's eyes. Thank God, I had an older man in my life. His name was Vernon. He gave me a lot of strength, and support while locked up. Today he is dead as well.

I finally moved to the west wing. There were three more weeks of living hell! All the girls talked about Mary's house, and how different it was from WCAC. I met this little girl named Kathy. She stood about 4' 10" tall and weighed about 105 pounds. She has light brown skin and had long black hair. She was very pretty. She and I got much closer. We were always together. She and I both were from Cleveland. She got caught with her boyfriend Darrius who was a car thief. The police had been looking for him for a while. Darrius was good when it came to stealing a car; he could have it in fewer than five minutes and be gone with your car. He was so good that the police had labeled him a menace to society. Kathy was sentenced to six months. She knew everything Darrius knew about stealing a car because he taught her. She also learned a lot just by being around him. She could steal a car just about as fast as he could; she even knew how to work on cars. The average young woman would not have any knowledge of these things. Finally, it was time to go to Mary's house after six weeks of hell. Kathy and I arrived at Ohio Reformatory for Woman together, ORFW. She and I were both scared but did not show it. She and I had never been locked up. We wore our street clothes from WCAC to ORFW. There were about twenty young women on the bus ride to Marysville Ohio Reformatory for Woman. Once we got to the farm, we had to walk the line as they called it. It was nothing more than the sidewalk. We had to get to the clothing exchange to get our new state outfits. We were looking all around. There were many cottages. That is where the women lived. Ohio Reformatory for Women, which is ORFW was out in the country way back in the woods. That was something I was not use to. There was nothing else around for miles and miles. I could not see anything but fields. I said to Kathy, "I do not know about this place." We heard cows mooing. At the time we did not see them, just heard them; it smelled like horseshit. Boy did it stink! As we were walking still trying to get to clothing exchange, we walked right passed all of the cottages. It was in the middle of March and nice outside. The yard was closed because they did not want the women out while we were walking, messing with the new women. The women were hanging out of the windows picking and choosing whom they wanted. Kathy had on a pair of blue jeans, red jacket, and red boots. I had on a black leather coat and a nice gray suit with heels. We had worn these clothes to court. One woman yelled out of the window saying, "The girl in the red boots is mine with her little fine self." Another voice yelled, "The one with the black leather and hells is mine. That was me, "I started turning around, checking out the other girls to see who else had almost the same thing on as me. No, one else did. "Kathy said, Dag, Doris, they are talking about me and you." We both said, "Girl, we are not on that dumb stuff." I said, "The bitches had better leave me alone and find them somebody that wants to be had." Kathy and I continued walking, side-by-side shaking in our shoes. All the whistling started. Some of the women were saying "You all do not know us yet, but in due time, you will." We did not know who was doing the talking. I did not care who it was. I said, "Girl, I know I will not be making it back home now for real because these women here are crazy."

We finally got to the clothing exchange. Thank God! Then I could get out my street clothes and look like everybody else. They issued us two red jumpers, two bras, two pairs of panties, two pairs of white socks, a pair of state shoes, two white blouses and a nice navy blue pea coat for the winter. After being processed in, we were told what cottage we would be in. Kathy and I were housed together but on different floors. We both were in Elizabeth Collage. Each Collage had its own name. Once there the C.O. gave us our room numbers. I was in a four-person dorm. Kathy was on the third floor with about ten women. After 5:00 P.M., Monday through Friday we could wear our street clothes on Saturdays and Sundays, we could wear street clothes all day. The clothes I had on when I got to the farm had to be sent home. We could not wear street clothes until our family sent us a clothes box. Some of the women had been locked up awhile would let some of the new women wear some of their clothes until they got their own but I was scared they would ask for something. Kathy and I said that after we went to our room to put our things away that we would meet in the hall of the second floor to go downstairs to the day room together.

We had missed lunch trying to get our things put up. There was nobody in the unit but the C.O. and us new women. The day room was not that big. It had lots of tables and chairs in the middle of the room and three benches on the wall where the new women were supposed to sit; however, we did not know that then, so we sat down, not picking any particular place; we just sat at a table. When the ladies got back from lunch, it was count time. The older ladies who had been at the prison told us they had count a lot during the day, mostly after each meal. The ladies said a count in the morning before breakfast, lunch, and dinner then again in the evening about 9:00 P.M. Another inmate walked up to us and said "Get up;" I said, "What?" She said, "You heard me. Get up." I said, "Why?" She said, "These are our seats." I said, "Well, I do not see any names on these seats." The one inmate was about to get up. I told her, "Wait a minute. They cannot just bully anybody around just because we're new." The old inmate said, Bitch, what is your name. I said, "It is not Bitch. Let me tell you something-- first, I am not your Bitch and nobody else's." I them said, "You do not know me, but that is bull shit what you are talking about. She then said to her friends, "I like her. She's got a little fire in her." I was not smiling; the woman was. I said, my name is Doris Williams and what is yours?" She laughed and said' "Joy." Then she wanted to talk as if she had some sense. She said, "Well Doris, let me tell you-- everybody in here's got a table and the entire new ladies sit on the wall." I said, "For how long?" She said, "Until somebody invites you to her table." I said, "What if no one does? "She said, "Well usually nobody stays on the wall for more than two weeks." I said, "Ok." I then said, "Why no one told us that in the beginning? I said, "You inmates just wanted to dog somebody;" I told her, "I was about ready to throw down" because girlfriend, I am not on that dumb stuff, She said, "Well Doris, I see you are not. I see you are for real and I like you, I said, "I do not play that. I am not into women," she laughed again and I said what is so funny, and she said, "You. "Doris, I was not talking about that. I am talking about you as a person, as a woman. I said, "OH, I'm sorry." She and I became good friends. She said she took a liking to me because I did not back down. I stood up to her. I told her that is the only way I know how to be which that is me and that I have been like that all my life. I also told her about that mess being not cool. The new inmates were already scared. People called me "crazy." I really did not see myself until I started typing my book, which I really would say anything of my mouth and I would fight at the drop of a pin. I was very outspoken on what I had to say. I did not care who I hurt because people did not care anything about my feelings. I felt like that for a very long time. I was angry at the world, and I did not know why. Thank God, I am not like that anymore; that was so ugly. I said exactly what I felt. I said to Kathy, "Maybe this stay here at Mary's house will not be too bad." Kathy was very outspoken as well. She "Shocked out" on probation after three months. I did not. I ended up doing nine months.

While at Marysville, I learned how to knit and crochet. I learned how to do one stitch and one stitch only. I was making Afghans big enough for bedspreads. I made one for just about everybody in my family in a different color. I felt they always used me for my talents. I was glad to do things because it came from my heart regardless of how badly my family talked to and about me.

I worked at Ohio Penal Industries (OPI) is what we called it. I sewed various flags, handkerchiefs, and banners. We did piece work just like a real sewing job. We worked eight hours a day, five days a week. I never knew who made the American flag. We had good times on holidays. We had activities and contests at our ball field. We played games such as who-al-loop, kick ball, softball, volleyball, and badminton. It was a lot of fun, considering we were young. I won first prize for who-al-looping. I received many Avon products, such as lipsticks, lotions, nail polish, skin softener and body power. We even had a special meal. Steak was a treat! I got respect from the inmates because I was myself, not trying to be something that I was not. I stayed to myself a lot, and minded my own business.

There was a big woman named Candace who had a very thick mustache just like a man. She was crazy about me, but I told her I had never had a woman and I was never planning to have a woman. That did not stop her from liking me. I told her we could be friends. I ate meals with her sometimes. At times, we walked around the yard and talked. I felt I needed someone to protect me somewhat, although I had no problem taking care of myself. I did feel better about being with a person that everyone respected and was scared of. The women could not understand what I had done to make those hard-core women like me as they did. She is dead as well. I was working at C.F.S, which was the kitchen. That was my very first job on the farm that I had when I got to Marysville, and I hated it. Candace found me to be funny. She never tried anything like that again because I stopped talking to her, and she was so hurt. She did not want me to stop talking to her. Shortly after that, I got my job in O.P.I. Sewing.

There was another woman named Blair who was also admiring me. I worked with her in O.P.I. I did not know what it was about me to make all of those women attracted to me. I was very pretty and I did not know it. Blair was in the life of gays, and I was not; and she knew that. She did not try to pressure me into anything. We were very cool, and all of the women on the farm were jealous of our relationship. Everybody was scared of her. No one understood how I could get away with doing so much stuff to her that the other women could not dare get away with. It was known that she lived a hard life. She was a very dark skinned woman with short hair like a man. She was built up more like a man than a woman was; she also had a bad- looking scary facial expression. She stood about 5'6". To me she was a very nice person who was doing some very big time for armed robbery. She had 3 to 15 years in the prison. There was no one on the outside to help her. She had to live off state pay, and that was not easy to do on twenty dollars a month; however, she had enough women on the farm that liked her and they wanted to take care of her. She as well is dead today.

My friend, Mr. Vernon, sent me a very nice clothes box. He had bought everything brand new. It pays to have a standby or a good friend because a friend in need is a friend indeed. That was a real blessing; God always had his angels watching over me. It was not anything that Vernon would not do for me. I was not in love with him; he was in love with me. I grew to love him because of the things he did for me. I was young; I thought he was supposed to do those things for me. He came to see me every month he used to pay somebody to bring him there to visit me which was a two-hour drive; most men would not have gone through all of that, but he showed me how much he really did care, and he made sure I did not want for anything. He kept money on my books; got me a brand new T.V. and I thanked God for him. I did not realize it then, but now I do he was there for me when I needed him the most. Mr. Vernon Green did my time with me. He is also dead.

I finally put in for a room change and got it. I did not like the dorm because the girls there did not show each other any respect. I got tired of looking at tits, and ass running around the room that was not mine, however, the women did not care. I got my single room, and I had a sink, a toilet, a dresser, a mirror, and a window in my room a twin size bed. Everything was so much better. I had my TV sitting on my dresser. If I did not want to be bothered with anyone, I did not have to deal with all the stupid stuff of the penitentiary. I stayed in my room as much as possible-- reading, eating, crocheting or just watching TV on weekends because we did not have to work. I went to church on Sundays. We also did not have to go to meals on the weekends unless we wanted to. We did have to attend count in the day room in our cottage.

As I was getting ready to go in front of an eight- panel board members; I was afraid. All the night before I tossed and turned. As I walked in the boardroom, they asked me to have a seat. I was shaking so bad my voice started cracking as I started talking. I said excuse me for that. They started asking me questions; I answered them the best of my ability and from my heart, I even started crying. They explained to me I was there for them to determine if I was going home or not and that they were going to review my case. I said, "Ok". I started praying, "Lord, please let the right words come out of my mouth." They asked me to tell them about my case that brought me there; they asked me how I felt now, and what have I learned since I have been incarcerated. All I knew was to tell the truth and how I really felt. I took a deep, deep breath; I started by saying." I made a mistake and I realize it. I know now that I have to live in society and do the right thing and that crime does not pay. I felt that I did not belong in a place like this; "I am too good of a person to throw my life away. There are many corrupt people here, and I really do not want to be around this crowd. I am going to try to do right, live right. I will not have to come back to a place like this. I have been scared straight. I'm very sorry, and I apologize deeply, and I have asked God to forgive me for my sins; also, I felt that God brought me to prison so that I could see if I did not straighten up this is how my life is going to be."

The board members looked at each other and nodded. I also think they knew in advance if they were going to give me my freedom or not. One chairperson who spoke for all the rest of them said, "Well Doris, we feel you have learned your lesson, and I do not believe you will be back, like most; they all come back in six months." "We are going to let you go home. Would you like that?" he said. I replied, "I like that, yes sirs, yes sirs, I promise I will never walk through these gates again." *Well, I stayed out for ten years.* I thought I had been scared straight. They all told me, "Good luck." I went around the table and shook everybody's hands. Then I started crying again. They told me I was free to go.

I could not thank them enough. As I was walking back to my cottage, a few of my friends asked me if I got my freedom or not. I said "Yes." Everybody told me that I was going to get my freedom, but I was not so sure. I said, "If it is the Lord's will." I went to the board in eight months; I went home a month later. Everyone was right. The board people gave me my freedom. Those nine months went passed fast. However, the last thirty days were a living hell. I got through it with no fights. Prison was not anything as I had thought it was going to be. I made it; I was getting ready to go home. I told some of my friends that I did not know how to act or dress anymore on the street. I felt as though I would not know how to do anything once back home. I was scared to get back on the street wondering how I would act at first, being out. I had thirty more days to try to get myself prepared for the outside world. There was paper work that had to be prepared. In the meantime I still had to go to work and do all of the other activates I would normally do on a daily basis. The last thirty days seemed like the longest. I left Blair my TV. Vernon was upset about that because he said he bought that for me. I told him she did not have anything or anybody to look out for her. I would have wanted someone to have done the same for me. That is how blessings come about, and I would get myself another TV once I was back on the street; he did not understand that. I was glad I could do a good deed for someone. Maybe God would bless me for that. Many other girls were asking me for different stuff. These girls did not have anything to do with me. There were times when I did not have food. They would not ask me if I wanted something to eat or share their food with me. They were looking out for self. Blair was not like that. She helped me out; yes, she did like me, but that did not matter. We were still friends. I guess you can say we were in a relationship without sex.

Dad's 84th birthday with Mother Chappell

CHAPTER FIVE

Being Home From prison

The day I left Marysville, the Farm, the c o came to get me at 8:00A.M. My family was there at 9:00 a.m. They said it took me a long time to come out of the facility. A nationwide check still had to be done on the computer before I was release. I had to take all my belongings over to the clothing exchange to check them out. They had to make sure that everything what I had been given when I came into the prison was returned. I went over to the visiting hall to be released. My mother and sister were standing there ready to take me home. I walked over to my mother and gave her a big hug, then my sister, and I started crying again. Mom said, "Jean, what are you crying for? I said what I said all the time. "I do not know," I said it seemed like those were my favorite words. I said, "I'm happy to be going home." My tears were happy tears. I asked my mom and sister how they got there. My mother did not drive at the time. Mom said, "Avery wanted to pick you up. "I asked, "Where is he?" Mom said, "Out in the car." I said, "Oh my God." My mother and sister helped carry my things outside. As we got closer to the car, he got out of the car and said, "Welcome home Baby," and gave me a big hug, then kissed me. I started crying again. He said, "It is going to be alright, baby, because I am going to take care of you.

As we were driving through the yard going to the exit, it was a nice day. I left on October 8, 1982. All the inmates were outside. My mother said, "Jean, are you going to wave bye to your friends? I said, "No, I do not have any friends." I said, "Get me out of here." I did not wave at anyone. I did not look back. I did not look side to side. My eyes were straight ahead because that is what I was told to do it was said that it was bad luck. I had said all my good byes the day before. I just wanted to get on the other side of the gate. That was my first time being In prison, and I thought my last. I said to my family, "These gates will never see me again. As we were heading home, Mom and Avery wanted to stop and get something to eat. I had told them that I would rather not. Mom said, "Oh Jean, it will be good for you." I was scared of being back in the streets with my freedom. We went on to the restaurant and ordered breakfast. I did not want anything to eat. They made me eat. The food even tasted funny to me. I did not have an appetite for real food. I was messed up in the head. We got back onto the road. Once they got me home everyone was there with open arms to welcome me home. I was tired and did not want to be bothered with anyone but Avery. I excused myself; and then I took him upstairs to the attic where my room was at my mother's house where I was living. I had it *f*ixed up before I left. Avery said that he would never let me go again, and if he had stayed with me, I would not have been in that place. I was so wild and vulnerable, I told him it was not his fault, and that for him not to blame himself. "It is over now." I had done the time. It was behind me. I just wanted to get my life back together. Avery said, "I will be here to help you do that." My mother had always been very fond of him. He was the only male that could spend the night with me without Mom saying anything. He stayed with me that night. He helped me unpack my little things that I had that Mom had packed up when I left.

I got my room back in living condition where I could find the things I needed. I was accustomed to having very little space. For the first month I was home, I was still acting and doing things as I was locked up. I had my room fixed up like in Marysville. I wore the same kind of clothes I wore in Marysville; I did not want to go outside of the house. Avery was right there for me. He tried to get me out to take me shopping, to dinner, or to a movie, and even out dancing. I said, "No". Avery respected that and just came to see me every day to spend time with me. My mother and I loved Avery Jones for the love he had for me. He has also passed on.

After a month, I started going out, doing things slowly. I was ready to look for a job. I still did not want to drive a car. Avery would take me around wherever I wanted to go. Vernon was there for me as well. I told Vernon that I was not driving yet. He would get rides to the house to see me. Avery used to drive my car around because it had been sitting while I was gone. Vernon was like a sidekick to me, a man who liked me and gave me lots of money to look pretty. However, my heart really was with Avery.

I found a job at a sewing factory doing piecework. Slowly I got used to being back in society. Avery started saying that I had changed so much. I did not see that and did not understand what he was talking about. Slowly, I was getting back onto my feet; he helped me get an apartment. He also started cheating around on me with other women. One night I went to his house, and he did not want to let me in, so I started hollering at the top of my lungs, he would not open the door. I told him, "I know you are in there." He still would not come to the door, I said, "If you do not let me in, I am going to get crazy. "You are with a woman." He *still* did not come to the door. His car was sitting in the driveway. I broke off his antenna. By the time I did that he had gotten his clothes on, and was at the front door saying, "Jean, what are you doing? I told him I knew what he was doing. He said, "I got company." I said, "I know and you are upstairs making love." I gave him his antenna and said, "I hate your ass and I walked away. "He was calling me to come back, but I did not. I got into my car and went home crying all the way. I still saw him from time to time after that, but our relationship had changed; it was never the same from that point on.

One night my girlfriend called me and said, "Jean, some of my friends are playing in the band at the "Reason Why." She wanted me to go with her to hear her friends play. I said, "I really was going to hang around the house because I have not been out of prison too long, and I still was not used of being out in the street." Pat begged and begged me to go. "OH please, Jean, you are not doing anything anyway. You need to put on some clothes and party a little." I said, "Ok, I will go." I went to pick her up, and we went on to the "Reason Why." I met my husband that night and did not know it. The man, Pat, was interested in played the base guitar. This other man kept on looking at me. I did not know him and Pat did not know him either. He was a friend to the men in the band. When we sat down, he kept on looking and looking at me; I mean he was staring at me so hard that I could not help but notice. He was not even blinking an eye. He was making me very nervous. I kept drinking, trying to ignore him. When the band went on break, I had to ask; "Who is that man who is undressing me with his eyes?" My friend, Pat, made her friend in the band introduce him to me. That is what he wanted; all of us were standing there on the stage. I got a little nervous again. I had my lighter in my hand and dropped it; "Mike" was his name, and he picked up the lighter from the floor for me with the quickest motion it made me smile; I had to ask him why he was looking at me so hard. He said, "I have to look at what I like you are so beautiful I just could not take my eyes of you." He made me blush. After the band started to play their last set, Mike invited Pat and I to sit with him. We were like in a booth, he and I sat on the same side; Pat was sitting across from us. He was boring; he did not have much to say. He was blushing as well. He was lost for words. I was trying to start a conversation because he was as fine as wine. Pat and I were doing most of the talking. He had this little miniature tape recorder; I had never seen anything like that in my life. I thought it was a toy of some kind because he kept playing with it. I should have known something was wrong with him then. He showed me how it worked and that it was not a toy. He sat there with us listening to that recorder as if we were not there. He did buy me a few drinks like he was supposed to do; therefore, he did know what to do. He asked me what I was going to do after leaving the club. I told him, "Take my friend home and go home myself." He said, "Well, I'm driving too. After you take Pat home, let's meet some-where to get something to eat." Now he wanted to get to know me. I said, "Ok." We met in front of Pat's house. He had to take some of the men in the band home. Little did I know that he had just gotten out the Army; and I had just got out of prison. He followed me home to drop off my car, and then I rode with him. He had a very nice car; he had play boy bunnies everywhere on his car, I said, "Oh, here goes another one," but he was getting my heart. I was wondering since he got out the army, what was he doing? We went to Denny's and had a very nice breakfast; we got a chance to talk. He had begun to open up to me a little, and he said he did not want to talk in front of Pat. This man looked so good that any woman would want to eat him up alive. He was buttering me up really good. He said, "He thought he was dreaming." I was too embarrassed at the time to tell him I just gotten out of prison. I was afraid I would chase him away, and I did not want to do that. I wanted to see him again. He told me he was a drummer and used to play with those men in the band that we were listening too. I said, "Oh, you are a musician;" he said, "Yes." He was looking for a band to play with. I liked being in his company but I would not let him know where I had just left from. As usual our relationship was nice at first; then he started standing me up a lot. He would not call to say he was not coming or that he had changed his mind; he just would not show up. He and I started getting closer, getting to know each other.

Finally, he took me to meet his family. His mother and grandmother lived next door to each other. I met his grandmother first. She was a very light- skinned woman about in her seventies with all white hair; she acted as if she did not like me. In time, it came about that she did not like me because I was too dark I guess. However, his baby's mother was about my color. His grandmother was very mean, and I was scared of her and I told him that. He said she was just crazy about him; he was her favorite grandchild and was jealous of any woman talking to him. He showed me his set of drums that he had set up in the dining room. His drum set was real pretty, white and gold. He showed me that he knew how to play them.

Me and Mike before marriage

Then he took me next door to meet his mother who was sitting on the couch. It looked like something was wrong with her. Mike introduced her as his mother. I know I was looking at her really funny. Her bust was very large; her waist and below were very small. She looked funny to me. Then I saw a wheelchair sitting in the living room. I did not know what to think. She was a very nice woman. She talked and talked to me. I told Mike he should have told me about his mother so it would not have been a surprise to me, and I would had of reacted differently. Mommy Palmer had multiple sclerosis of the liver; she had suffered with that disease since she was four years old, and her mother had always been very close around to protect her. Mike's mother was one of the kindest persons I know. She did not want people to look at her as a person who cannot walk. She did a lot of things and more than a person who can walk. I admired her for who she was and how she got around. She had four children, three boys and one girl; Mike was the oldest. Her children sometimes ran over her. After a few months, his mother and

I got tight. I finally told him that I had just gotten out of prison when I met him. I had to tell him before our relationship got too far. After getting that out, I felt better within myself. He asked me about what I done, and I explained everything to him. He said he did not like me for my past; he liked me for what he saw in me, and for who I was. That was such a good feeling when he said that to me. It made me feel so much better knowing that he understood. My prison stay was something I did not talk about to anyone or everyone. That part of my life I wanted to bury. He finally got back with his old band. They were good. I used to attend all of their seasons. He could sing. Something changed with him. He started dogging me. I knew he had fallen in love with me, and he did not want to admit that so he started affairs with many different women, "Dogging me out" as if I had done something to him. I was still seeing him at times, but he wanted his cake and eat it too. I would follow him. I would go to different people's houses in the band who he hung around with; I was "cool" with the wives of the other men in the band. One time at the after hour place where we went after the band got finish playing, I saw him there with another woman. He asked me why I was following him. I told him I was not, that we just happened to be at the same place, but for real, I was following him because I had fallen in love with him. He used to act as if he hated me. That was a cover up, for his real love, he had for me, but I did not know that at the time. Every time I went around him, he got very upset, so I poured it on. This one time his band was playing and he would not talk to me. I said, "Find." I would buy all the band members drinks. I would tell the bartender that the drummer was not to get anything from me. I used to dog him back every chance I got when he started that dumb mess. I was talking to this other man named Sam who worked on my car, he was very much in love with me as well but my heart was for Mike. Sam was very jealous, and a drunk. I told him I do what I want to do when I get ready. No man was going to tell me what to do because he was not my man or husband. My mother instilled that in me. I did not have a husband at the time. I was my own woman. I thought he was good at the work he did, but I did not know he was rigging my car. Therefore, no one could come behind him and work on it. My engine had gone out.

Sam said, "No problem. I will put another one in your car." I thought it was pretty nice to have him around. I got what I wanted and needed from him. He just drank too badly for me. He told me to stay off the freeway with the car. He knew I had to go on the freeway East 270th street and Euclid Avenue in Cleveland, Ohio, which was across town from where I did all of my business and partying. When I went to the after hour spot which was on East 86 street on Euclid Avenue, it was faster for me to get home going on the freeway. He knew I took the freeway to get many places.

One night we were at the after hour spot where we usually went when Mike and the band had finished playing. The door attendant sent someone in to tell me someone wanted me outside. It was Sam. He wanted me to go with him; I told him I was not going anywhere with him because he followed me plus he was drunk. He left and came back in an hour. Mike asked me what he wanted; I told him. Sam sent for me again. Mike said, "The nigger better not be starting any mess with you." Mike would not let me go outside again.

Sam sent me a message back and said that if I did not come to see what he wanted, he was going to bust my windows out of my car. I told Mike; he told me to stay inside and he would take care of the situation. Mike said, "I am not going to let him mess with your car." I do not know exactly what happened outside, but Mike would not let me go home by myself that night. He used to carry a gun, and he was not afraid to use it. I said to him, "What are you going to do? You got that woman with you." He said, "I am going to take her home and meet you at your apartment." I said, "Ok." Sam said how he was going to mess up Mike and I. Mike was afraid for my safety to go home alone. He had been in the army. I took the freeway home from the after hour spot. I got two exits before mine when the car started running hot on me. It was still dark, about 5 a.m. It was just starting to get light. I pulled over to the side of the road, and then the car died out completely. I was scared, and I was scared to get out of the car. I said, "Oh Lord, what am I going to do?" I sat there in the car for minutes. I could not call Mike because we did not have cell phones then. I knew he was at my house waiting for me and wondering what was taking me so long to get to my house. I finally got out of the car and started walking; it was a very hot summer night. I was dressed very nicely in a black dress, gold heel, with a black and gold purse with gold jewels. As I started walking, a very nice couple who was dressed very nicely looking as if they were coming from a party themselves, they picked me up and said "That must be your car on the side of the road." I said "Yes" I was looking so pretty. It was on a Saturday night. I had taken my shoes off so I could walk faster. The man driving said, "We will drop you off; we are going right passed where you live at." The nice couple dropped me off right in front of Mike's L.T.D car sitting on the street in front of my apartment. I could not thank the couple enough. I asked them what I owed them; the man said nothing. I said, "Let me at least give you a few dollars for gas." The man said, "We were glad to help a sister."

The first thing Mike said was, "Jean where is your car.?" I said, "On the side of the freeway." He said, "We have to go back and get it;" I said, "I will call AAA." He said, "Before we do that and go to get your car, I want to know who that person is sitting back there in a car looking like Sam." Mike had already scanned the parking lot because he just did not trust Sam. We drove back to the parking lot; we got out of the car to get a really good look. I said, "That is Sam." He was asleep. Mike wanted to wake him up. I said, "No, we are not going to get in trouble. I will call the police;" they were there within 10 minutes. Euclid, Ohio, where I was living did not play. The police woke Sam up. I told them we were out partying and Sam threatened to mess my car up. Then he was waiting for me to come home, but Mike would not let me come home by myself. Thank God, because there was no telling what Sam would have done to me. The police checked out all three of us. Mike and I were clean. Sam had a warrant out on him, so he went to jail. After he got out of jail, he called me to say he was going to mess up Mike. I told Sam, "You tell him yourself." I handed Mike the phone. They exchanged words. Mike told him that he would be right there with me and he did not leave from that day until we got married.

Mike moved in with me, and I had to stop seeing the other men I was seeing. He never left me. He, too, stopped seeing the women he was seeing, and he ended up asking me to marry him. Marriage was the furthest thing from my mind. I started laughing, he said, "What's so funny?" and I said, "You." "You are serious?" He said, "Very much so, and it is not funny." I apologized for laughing but, "Mike, what do you expect? You have had me chasing you for a year," I said. "You moved in with me because of Sam's mess. Now you want to marry me. Your mother had to make you first come over to my house. I just do not believe you. We talked about the situation. I told him I was not going to make any plans until I got a ring because it was just hard to still believe he wanted me. I did not even tell my parents until I got the ring. Mike was not going to make me look like a fool anymore; he had a ring for me that next month. It was not a real expensive ring, but it was a ring. I jumped up, grabbed and kissed him all over I said, "You are serious? It is for real." I told my mother and the rest of the family I was getting married. Nobody could believe that I, Jean was finally getting married because I was so wild. No man could really do anything with me. I would not listen to anyone, but I was ready to listen to him. Anything Mike wanted, and the way he wanted, it was done; I was willing to do. We set the date for a year away, which was August 10, 1985. I could not believe it myself because I thought God was not going to ever grant me a husband. I really thought no man would have me for his wife because marriage came so late in life for me. I was thirty when I got married.

CHAPTER SIX

My Wedding Planning

I planned my wedding myself because I wanted it big. I knew it was going to take me some time to pull it together. This was my first marriage. It was a family tradition that we stay with our husband and take the bitter with the sweet. My wedding colors were light blue, my maid of honor who was my baby sister wore royal blue. The men's shirts matched the ladies dresses, and all the men and boys had on white tuxedos. My flower girls wore light blue. I had eight bride maids and four flower girls. Two threw flowers and the other two carried my train. Most of the wedding party was family, either my husband's or mine. I had four ushers. All my family from all parts of the world attended my wedding. My wedding was a beautiful sight to see. It was one of the most beautiful weddings you ever laid your eyes on considering we were poor and my dress was beautiful as well. My train was over 20 feet long and had pleats all the way to the end. It fit tightly at the bust and the waist. The neck area and the sleeves were see-through. I went to Atlanta Georgia, for a week to find a hat because I could not find one in Cleveland that I liked. Even then, I had to search store after store to find a hat that I liked. My sister, Ola, who lived in Atlanta Georgia, got tired of taking me to store after store. She was ready to give up on my hat and me. I said, "Ola this is special to me, and you have to help me find my dream hat. "She said, "Ok Jean, one more mall." I agreed one more mall, and I saw the hat in the window I wanted I had to have it! It was like a half of a hat that just fit in the center of my head. It had beads coming down in the front and on the sides. It was beautiful. I had never seen anything like that before in a wedding hat. I had to go inside the store to inquire about it. When the saleslady showed me the price, I almost choked. I looked at my sister and she looked at me. I told the saleslady, "Thank you very much." We left the store, went out into the center of the mall, and had a seat. My sister said, "You really like that hat don't you?" I said, "Yes, but I am not going to pay three hundred dollars for it." I was finished sopping for that day. I was sick. I went to my sister's house and called my fiancé in Cleveland. I told him that I had seen a hat and it was so beautiful, but it was three hundred dollars. He said, "Baby, if that is your dream hat, go ahead and get it. That is what you went down there for, isn't it?" I said, "Yes, but it is three hundred dollars." He said, "Don't you have the money?" I said, "Yes, and more. "He convinced me that my wedding day only comes once. A big smile came on my face. I had to tell my sister Ola that we had to go back and get that hat. I wanted that it. With my luck, they would not have it any longer. I should have gotten it then. Ola called the boutique to make sure it was still there. It was! My sister told the sales clerk who we were, the sales clerk remembered us. My sister told the saleslady I was going "Nuts," afraid the hat would not be there. The sales clerk told my sister she could tell I really wanted that hat because my face lit up like a Christmas tree; I thought my desire for the hat could not be seen. The sales clerk said she will put it up until the next day, and it would have my name on it. I could not wait until the next day. My sister had to take me back to the mall that same evening because the wait was eating me up inside. The sales clerk told me she could tell I was going to be a very beautiful bride. "You are a special woman," she said. I thanked her for all the lovely comments.

One of my wedding pictures

My husband Mike and I

I got onto the airplane within the next two days, heading back to Cleveland. I was so very happy. I had found that special hat for my special day. I could not go back home empty handed without a hat. That was the whole purpose. My sister was tired of running me around and told me she had never known that I was so hyperactive. My mother though it was a beautiful hat and one of my aunts liked it as well.

However, another aunt said I was a fool because there was no way she would pay that kind of money for a hat to wear one day. I told her that she was not me. She went on to tell me that nine times out of ten that he and I would probably not even stay together. I felt she was "Burning bread on me." After the wedding I told her that I could and would take the veil off and just wear it as a white hat because it was a very sharp hat, and I was a "Hat-wearing sister". I starting wearing hats from my mother and until today I still love my hats. That is how my mother raised my sisters and I. We always wore a hat to church. I told my aunt that was a terrible thing to say that we were not going to stay together. I asked her how she knew. She said, "Most people don't." I told her just because her marriage ended up in divorce does not mean it will happen to me. I got very upset with her comments. My shoes also were white, and the toe and heel were out. Now everything was out of the way, and I could move on to other business dealing with my wedding. My mother had one of her friends make my cake. My mother and I went to her house to see some of her work. She did very good work. That was the way she made her living. The woman asked me what I wanted. I told her my husband was a drummer, and I wanted a few layers heart shaped. I had an eight-layer cake. I did not see the cake until the reception. It was so beautiful. It had four layers coming down in front of each other with poles between the layers—one on each side with ladders coming up to meet the one stack in front. Then the cake had little statues of men and women on the ladders; the women were dressed in light blue, and the men were dressed in black.

My wedding cake, my bridesmaids and flower girls

My grand dad and I

There was an extra layer with a heart shaped on the side with a drummer boy on it. My husband got a big "kick" out of that. The reception was very nice. I got drunk. Actually, I was drunk at the wedding. While coming down the aisle, I was tripped up in my dress some kind of way. I think the two little girls who were carrying my train did not have it held correctly or something. We had a video tape made as well along with our wedding pictures; when I went to pick the pictures up from the studio, the lady just kept talking about my husband and how handsome he was. She kept on saying that, and how much she loved my dress. She did not say anything about me, so I was very anxious to see the tape. My husband was drunk as well. He did not have on socks. A person could not tell he was drunk as I was. Of course, I started crying, walking down the aisle. For some reason I had this piece of Kleenex in my hand. My wedding was over an hour late getting started. I was angry. Then they told me my husband had forgotten the license, and he had to go back home to get it. We lived about twenty miles from the church. I was "On pins and needles" thinking Mike was not going to show back up. My mother and all my bride's maids were trying to keep me clam, but I was drunk. By the time I got down the aisle to my husband, the tears were pouring down my face. I pulled out my Kleenex from under my sleeve and wiped some of my tears; Mike walked over to me and got me from my grandfather who gave me away. Mike was smiling, and he said, "Are you all right? I nodded smiled back at him, and said to him, "Yell. " Mike kept on looking at me smiling. He reminded me of when we first met and he said that "He could not take his eyes off me." Now we were in front of the preacher. My nose was running really badly from all the crying I had done while walking down the aisle. I was trying hard to get myself together. The cameraman and the video man were both right there in my face, shooting everything that was going on. I said, "O Lord, I got to blow my nose.", but I really was trying to suck it back up inside of me; that did not work. After a while this loud noise came from me. The entire wedding party looked at me, but I acted as if nothing had happened. I blew my noise. I felt better after that. My husband looked at me and shook his head. I looked at him and smiled; we both smiled at each other. Then I was ready to continue with the wedding. I even messed up on my vows; I stumbled through some of the words. My husband smiled about that. We were looking at each other; I was talking loud enough where everyone could hear me. He was not. My mother and father were sitting in the front row, and they said they did not hear Mike say a word of his vows. Altogether, my wedding was very lovely, August 10, 1985, I got the tape and pictures to always remind me. We had a white stretch limousine with a nice bar inside.

We did not get the reception taped because money was low. When I got ready to throw my bouquet, I threw it, and hit the ceiling and then the floor, so I threw it again. The second time was successful. My girlfriend, Donna, caught it, and she said she probably will not ever get married; my sister's boyfriend at the time caught the garter belt. Today he is my brother-in-law. My sister and he got married ten years after me. She copied off of me because her color was light blue as well. We had spent so much on the wedding, the reception, and the video tape that we were flat broke. We got some very lovely gifts and over a thousand dollars in cash; we had to pay bills with some of the money. Surprisingly, my husband's family did not buy us anything. We did not even get a gift from any of them; that hurt me to my heart. I thought my mother in law was better than that. Mike had a daughter who was four years old at the time. His grandmother was still crazy about his baby's mother. Mike's mother said Mike's baby's mother was still like a daughter-in-law to her.

My husband was doing security guard work at the time when we got married which did not pay much money, and he kept changing jobs due to him being laid off. Thus, Mike decided to go back into the army; at the time, I was in school, and I wanted to graduate from computer school. He re-enlisted and got sent to Germany. My graduation from computer school was in November of 1986; I however decided not to join him until Christmas 1986. I got my certificate, and I graduated with honors. After graduation, I got a job at Light Tung as an order taker during the holiday season. By my birthday being the day after Christmas, I gave myself a birthday and going away party. All my co-workers, students who I had gone to computer school with and other friends were there. It turned out to be a very nice event considering I gave it for myself. When I told my husband about my party, he got angry at first, and said that he was not there to help me celebrate the occasion. I told him to be happy for me because I was coming over there with him. This news was a surprise to him. I decided not to wait for the government to send me a ticket. I saved my money and sent myself. Mike was happy to hear that. I had my plane ticket in my hand.

CHAPTER SEVEN

My Years in Germany

I was due to leave Cleveland on December 27, 1986, at 7:30 p.m. I had said all of my good-byes to family and friends. I was not going over there to stay, so I thought. I had said I would stay there three weeks to a month. I had four suit cases with me. Two were small, one large, and one medium suitcase. When I got to the plane that evening, everything was Ok. I ended up getting my military discount on my airfare. I flew from Cleveland to New Jersey. Once I got to New Jersey, I had problems concerning my flight on to Germany. I called my husband, and he said he did not have anywhere for me to live because they still had him living on the post. He told me to go back home and wait until the government sent for me. I said I am not; there was no way I was going back to Cleveland. I did not go that far to turn around and go back home. I said, "Baby, please work on It." I stayed in the officers' hotel in New Jersey. I was only paying eight dollars a night for a week before I could finish my journey. I found my way to the P.X. I did not have a military I.D. yet, but I had my passport and all my husband papers showing that I was his wife. Some places on the post I could not get into without an I.D. card. I stayed in the hotel in my room a lot and ate a lot of pizza and talked to my husband just about every day.

I thank God that I had enough money to carry me over. Mike kept telling me to go back home. I said, "Baby, I have been here in Jersey a week, and I am boarding the plane. He had to try to arrange on his end somewhere for me to stay. I said, "I will call you and let you know what time I will be arriving in Germany." I am on my way, I went over to the airport, checked my bags in, and came to find out; they told me I could not board with four suitcases. Only three pieces of luggage were allowed. I said what I am supposed to do with my one suitcase; they told me they did not know. I walked away crying and took a seat. This man walked up to me and said Ms. I see you need help. He was standing around and heard the conversation. He told me to put a dollar into the locker; when my husband and I could return to this point to see if my stuff was still in the locker. I had nothing to lose, so I took the man's advice. I put one suitcase into the locker and turned the key. I was ready to check in again this time everything was "Ok." I prayed and prayed for God to keep my stuff safe until we came back that way. I flew from New Jersey to Germany. It was an eight-hour flight. Before the plane took off, I called Mike and told him what time I should be getting into Frankfurt airport. Mike said, "Ok I will be there." That was the longest flight I had ever been on in my entire life. Once I got off the plane, I did not know what to do, so I followed the crowd of people because I did not see my husband. I looked all around and did not see him anywhere. The crowd of people went downstairs to get their luggage; I followed them and got my luggage as well. The people were getting buggies, and I needed a buggy; so I went to get one as well. I put my four quarters into the machine, and my money kept coming back to me. This one woman told me that I needed marks. I asked her where I could get them. In a very strange, English- speaking American voice, she directed me where to get the marks. I liked her ascent. I used the phone to see where Mike was; but he did not answer the phone. I sat down and cried as well as prayed. An hour had passed, and he still was not there to pick me up. While waiting on my husband, I knew I needed marks. I went to exchange some of my money into marks. As I walked out of the bank, the first person I saw was my husband. I ran over to him and gave him a big kiss and hug in front of everyone. Mike was smiling at me. He looked so good to me in his uniform. He had a few of his boys with him. Then I stepped back, punched him in the chest, and said, "Where were you?" His boys said, "Damn man, she's got some punch on her. "I said, "I have been here for over an hour; you knew I would have been scared out of my mind." I also said, "Mike where were you when I got off the plane? He replied, "Wait a minute, baby I had problems getting off work and finding someone to bring me here. Aren't you glad to see me? I said, "Yes." He told me to stop fussing. "I am here now." I forgot about everything. I was so glad to see him. I had never been so glad to see my husband in my life. He then said, "Let's get out of here." We went to the car. Those little cars over there looked so funny to me, but they were cute. He said he was due back at work. I said, "What are you going to do with me?" He said, "Well, Baby, I have got to find a room somewhere." He did find a room that was so cold. The Germans like it cold, and I did not. In addition, however, the room was very expensive, Mike told me not to worry about anything. He got me settled in the room and stayed with me for an hour talking, and we were glad to see one and another. We had sex, and then he had to leave. Mike's sex was not that good, but we worked on it. We brought our sex up to standard for the both of us. He knew how to please me; and that was what counted. I unpacked my things and turned on the TV, but I could not understand a word they were saying because it was all in German so I turned it off. Then I started to look out of the window. Oh, my God, the view was beautiful. I had never been outside of the United Stated; everything was so different and pretty. The houses were sitting high up on hills and many of the streets were brick. The little police cars made a funny noise.

Germany houses in Gilhousen

Me on the streets of Germany in Gilhousen

The police were called poliza meaning German police. They were dressed funny to me like something a person would see on TV or if they were in the military. I saw all of that just walking around the area. I did not want to go too far for fear of not finding my way back to the hotel. Once I got back, I tried to lie down and take a nap, but it was too cold in the room for me. I got up and went downstairs to ask the woman at the front desk if I could please have another blanket. She gave me a real thick comforter. I then went back upstairs and went to sleep. My husband came back to the hotel after getting off work; he had to wake me up.

He wanted me to get dressed to take me out on the town and around his friends. I got up and dressed and he took me on post. I had never seen anything like that in my life. I had never been on a military base before everything on post looked old. All of the buildings on the post were an old gray brick that looked dirty. Once inside the building, they looked very nice. They had the N.C.O. Club inside, and there was a bar and a dance floor, dining area, and a cashier window where the solders went to cash their checks. Everyone went there to eat, drink, and dance at night. They were playing music as well. By this time, I was tired and having jet lag from the flight, but my husband did not want to take me back to the room. He wanted me to hang with him, so I did. He filled me up with drinks until I was drunk and then told me I was safe. I did not feel my tiredness anymore. I was "Tripping out" on their taxi cabs which were very expensive Rolls Royce's.

The PX on the post had a lot of different clothes. The commissary was the food store. It took me a while to get used to calling the right name to the right place such as, the commissary, the PX, the NCO Club, and money marks. Their marks looked like play money to me, and I did not want to deal with it. I was getting the coins and paper marks mixed up.

We went off the post to one of his friend's house. Their house was very American, and reminded me of home. I found out that their toilets flushed funny. I could not find out how to flush the toilet. I had to call my husband. I looked all over for the handle and could not find it. My husband came in; I said, "Baby, where and how in the world do you flush the toilet?" He said, "Look up." I did, saying what now. Mike` said, "Look Jean, I want you to find it." I looked up again and above the toilet bowl up in the air was a chain to pull to flush the toilet. Something told me to pull the chain. I did and the toilet flushed. I said," This is incredible," I had never seen anything like that before in my life. There were many different things about Germany that I was not accustomed to. I got the hang of things fast though. I told my husband I did not want to deal with the monopoly money; it looked too much like play money. The paper marks were very large, much larger than American paper dollars.

I developed this black and white picture of me, barriers in background Gilhousen Germany outside of Frankfurt

After being in Germany a while, I told Mike that I did not want to go back to the States. My place was with him. He did not put up a fight with me about staying. Since I had went over to Germany on my own he had to get what is called orders cut recognizing me as his wife so I could get the wife benefits to stay in Germany with my husband. We did not get the opportunity to get government housing because he was only an E-3 at the time of him re-entering into the Army he had to be an E-4. Therefore, we found a real nice place off of the post which was not too far. Sometimes I used to walk to the post. Government housing was called Economy housing. I really did not want to live in government housing because the army always came to inspect at any time they wished. The government was telling the people who were in Government housing what and what not to do, they could not put anything on the walls. I did not want to live like that. The only advantage in Government housing quarters was that a soldier's family did not pay any rent. That would have saved us a lot of money. All military families lived right together. It reminded me of the ghetto, and I wanted no part of that. Then they kept up too much noise for me. Mikes and I was more private people.

A German woman rented us a studio apartment; it was little but furnished, there was a small living room, a small bedroom with the bed on the floor, a dresser, and a closet. The closet was called a "Shrunk." It was big enough to fit the entire wall. There were shelves where we could put sweaters or other things. The other long side was for hanging clothes. Mike and I both had a side of the closet that looked just alike. The living room furniture was not the best, but I made a cover for the couch and it was find. Most of the apartments were furnished. A person could sit in the living room and see directly into the bedroom because there were no dividers or no door there. I got some thick beads and hung them there which were better than having nothing hanging up. The kitchen was across the hall. That was different to me. We had to go out of the living room and the house and go across the hall for the kitchen. It was as big as the living room and the bedroom put together. The Germans has a very funny odor about themselves. They would buy this stuff at the store and wash themselves with it. It was like a wash form bath solution, but to me, it was nothing. The women would put perfume on top of their "Not to good Smell body." German woman are known for leather. I had gotten a few pieces from over there that I will never see anywhere in the United States.

Some of my cermines I made in Germany

Jean out on a date

My first job in Germany was in the N.C.O club. I made change for the slot machine and cashed checks. I had a little booth that was nice. I was a well-liked person because I was very dependable. During that time my husband got a call from his family saying his grandmother was very ill and the doctors did not think she was going to make it. Mike got a thirty-day leave. The family told Mikes' grandmother he was on his way because he was her favorite grandchild. They saw her smile when she was told that. She was trying to hold on until he got there, but she was just too weak. We left Germany at once. When we got to the States, we went straight to the hospital; she had been dead an hour. Mike cried and cried because he did not get to see her for the last time alive. The funeral was very sad. Afterword's, everyone gathered at Mike's mother's house, not only because of the funeral but they had not seen him in over a year. There were many of his old friends who had stopped by to wish their condolences, and out of all the people come popping up was Cherry, Mike's daughter's mother and his daughter Toya. Mike told Cherry she could leave "Toya with us and he and I would bring her home." She said "Ok". She still sat around for a while trying to be noisy, asking Mike how long we will be home. He told her that we would be home for thirty days. It seemed like she was stopping by the house at least twice a week. She even found out we were staying with Mike's mother while we were in town. Those were very long thirty days. We both were ready to get onto the plane to go back to Germany. The army paid for the both of us to fly round trip. I had to put up with Cherry coming by the house telling us how good we looked together. We knew that and really did not want to hear that from her. I did not like her because she thought she was better than me, and tried to talk down to me in a very sneaky way. She was jealous I was with Mike and she was not. She made a statement on how much she loved my ceramics that I learned how to do while in Germany. She was just trying to start a conversation and be noisy to get into our business. I was sending a lot of my ceramics pieces home to my family and my husband's family that I was making while in Germany. Cherry had said how I should try to go into business because my work was so beautiful. I had started a little business selling my ceramics to soldiers especially around Christmas time. I made nice money. Everybody wanted gifts to send home to their loved ones. We also spent a lot of time at my mother's house while home in the States. Mom loved to cook and we ate dinner and spend the evenings with her almost every day. We also spend a lot of time with his daughter, Toya, and my niece, Toni, who were about the same age of eight years old; we took them to, the amusement parks and the zoo. They both had a lot of energy. We did make our thirty days home enjoyable. Towards the end of our thirty days, the night before we left Cleveland heading back to Germany, my mother gave us a going away party because there was no telling when they would see us again. All of our friends and family were there. Memories were made that night that we took back to Germany with us.

I remembered, about my suit case I had left in New Jersey, I told Mike we had to go back there on our way back to Germany. He said, "Ok, but your suitcase probably not there Jean, after all this time." That was something I had to find out for sure for myself. We flew from Cleveland to New Jersey. The flight was good and short. Once in Jersey, we went straight to the place where I had left my luggage. I put my key into the locker and opened the locker, and my things were still there. My husband was surprised after all those months my luggage was still there. I was happy; things were just as if I had left it. I hollered and said "Yes Lord thank you.

We had to stay in Jersey over night because the flight for Germany did not leave until the next day. We spend the night in the same officer's club hotel when I went through by myself. "The desk clerk remembered me and said, "Glad to see you again, Mrs. Palmer, and glad to see you have your husband with you this time. There were many military people to board the plane. The desk clerk gave us the same room I had when I was traveling alone.

That next morning we got up early, ate breakfast, and went to where the plane was going to depart from. The only plane I saw out in the field was an army plane, a big DC10. It was multi-colored green, just like the army uniforms. The plane did not have any windows. I said, "Oh my God, we are going to die." My husband said, "No, we are not; we will be OK. I had never been on an airplane like that before. My husband said that is the kind of plane, which carries the tanks, and it transports the soldiers when they go to war. That was the most boring and longest flight I had ever been on. When we boarded the plane, it was very small inside; it could only hold about twenty passengers. I said to my husband, "The plane looks so big from the outside," which it was. The tanks and soldiers took up the space. We did not get anything to eat on the flight. The plane did not seem like it was going as fast as the regular 747. I said, "Baby; I think I am really going to be sick." The army had given Mike some earplugs, he gave me candy and gum. The plane was very, very loud.

Once back in Germany, I called my boss from the airport because we did not have anyone to pick us up. Winston, who was my boss, came to get us. He was a Sergeant First Class in rank, which is an E-7. My boss was glad we were back. He wanted me to work that night because he was short of help in the club. I told him I had just gotten off that multi-green bird which was the army plane; he laughed. I was tired, but Winston said he really needed my help. He kept on trying to convince me he needed my help, he said, I could go home, rest a few hours, and he would even pick me up. I finally said, "OK, I will work." When my husband and I got home; I unpacked, and cooked us something to eat. I laid down for an hour; got up, took a shower, and got ready to go to the club. My husband came later because he wanted to see his friends. I called Winston and told him he could come and pick me up. Mike and I did not have a car yet. We were planning to get my car shipped over there. I told my boss, I did not think I would have had the strength to work after just getting off an eight hour flight. I did it and felt good about helping out.

For the fourth of July that year the club was planning on having music, dancing, drinking, and they were selling dinners, ribs, chicken, potato salad, baked beans, greens, corn on the cob, and corn bread. This was for the single soldiers who did not have any family over there. They wanted me to help with the cooking. I helped from 10:00 a.m. to 3:00p.m. My husband was at the club with me on the holiday. Later that night we went out dancing in Frankford. I wanted to go to Frankford because I had heard so much about it and the red light district.

I met another one of my husband's friend's wife she was a nice woman; she was a bit on the large size, she and I got along pretty well. We started going out and being together some times. I was at her house one day because I had not seen her in a while. She opened the door and told me to come in. Once inside the house, I got a really good look at her. I said, "Girl, what in the world happened to you? She told me to be quiet and come into the bedroom because her husband was home. As I walked through the house, I passed him, I spoke, and he spoke back to me. We went into the bedroom and closed the door. Of course he knew she was telling what had happened. I was Debbie's best friend in Germany. Her husband had jumped on her. Both of her eyes were black, and her face was very swollen. She and I continued as if nothing had happened. She stayed close to the house looking like that. She really did not want to go out in public to let everyone see what had taken place. I checked on her every day either by telephone or I stopped by to see how she was doing.

Black marketing was a big thing in Germany. I thought black marketing was dealing with babies being sold. I was wrong. Black marketing is anything Americans get and sell to Germans, such as American cigarettes, meat, liquor, and coffee which the government rationed to each American family was issued two ration cards. Every time we went to the store to buy those items, our ration card would get a punch for that week. We were allowed to buy only two cartons of cigarettes a month per person. Germans were in love with Winston, Kool, and Marlboro cigarettes, which were their three favorites. Like others I started Black marketing one time a German man told me to bring him some steaks and hamburger meat. I had taken over my friends business. I got introduced to German men to buy and order product from me. They kept me very busy. Mike knew how to get the ration cards. We bought one hundred cards for a dollar each. If he would have gotten caught, that would have been his stripes, and they probably would had kicked him out of the army. I did not mind buying the cards because it was only going to make me money. The Germans paid top dollar for what they wanted. I did not mind selling them anything; the money was really good. It did not take me long to learn about the marks (German currency).

We had been looking around for a new place to live, but I saw nothing that I liked. I started meeting people at work. This one girl who I worked with, invited me to her house, and I fall in love with her apartment. It was furnished with real nice furniture. It had a nice living room set, big bedroom, with a big bed, and a kitchen there in the apartment, so we did not have to go across the hall way to get to the kitchen. I asked my girlfriend how much her rent was; she said "Four hundred and eighty marks a month." I said "That is a lot," but I still wanted to move there because our apartment that we had was a dump compared to the new place. However, the apartment we had, we were paying only two hundred and fifty marks a month. I went home and told Mike about the apartments; I had to take him to go and see it. He loved the apartment as well; he said, "Jean it is doubled from what we were paying now" I said, "I know, but it is worth it." It took me about a week to convince him that I really wanted that apartment. I told him that I was also working to help out paying the bills. We arranged to see the property owner to look at an empty apartment. At the time, there were not any empty apartments. All military families lived in the apartments. The property owner said all the apartments were the same. My husband and I went to my girlfriend's house; he liked it a lot. The property owner said that there was a family moving out in a month. We went ahead and paid the security deposit and the first month rent. I was happy that the apartment was ours. I was so pleased with my husband for agreeing to move to a better location.

That next month the property owner called us to let us know the apartment was empty and that we could move in at our earliest convenience. I could not wait; we moved right away. It was a struggle to pay the rent because our income had taken on a four hundred dollar car note. Our income had taken a down fall.

The Criminal investigation department (CID) was looking at me. I had to almost completely stop Black marketing. Mike and I had known somebody had tipped off CID and the MP's of what I was doing because all of a sudden I got a phone call. The voice said, "I am calling for Palmer, and the message is whatever you've got there, get rid of it; they are on their way," and hung up the phone. I said, "Who is this?"

but they had already hung up. I sat on the couch for a minute and said to myself, "Move your ass, Dummy! They just gave you a tip." I had all kinds of stuff in the house that I had not gotten rid of yet. I had to find a safe place to keep it. We had a storage bin in the basement. I thought to myself, "Do not take it down there because that probably would be one of the first places they would search." I took the cigarettes and all the ration cards upstairs and asked my girlfriend to keep them for me. "Please," I said, "They have no reason to search your apartment." My friend, Sharon, was very noisy, and she wanted to know what was going on. I said, "I will tell you later, I do not have time right now." She said "Ok". I'll be dog gone. It was not five minutes later there was a knock on my door. I opened the door; it was CID in regular clothes, with two military police, I said yes, my I help you, come on in I said. We went to the living room and I asked them if they wanted a seat. They said, No." we will stand, and I said, "Well, what can I help you people with?" They were looking all around the house as far as their eyes could see. I said, "What is it you guys are looking for?" They said, "Mrs. Palmer, we know you are black marketing; you might as well give us the ration cards." Of course, I said, "I do not know what you are talking about." They said, "Sure, you don't. If you do not mind can we look around? I said, "Be my guess, but I do not want my house torn up." They went into the kitchen and opened all the cabinets; there were two Carlton one Salem Light, and one Newport cigarette. They asked me if that was all of my cigarettes. I said, "Yes sir." The man said, "Oh, come on, we know you got lots more than that." Once again I said, "I have told you all what I have, I have no idea what you're talking about and why are you here. Whoever told you those lies maybe you need to check them out." CID continued to check my apartment and found nothing, and they did not tear up my house. They were upset; they said I got a call, I said, "A call about what?" "No sir," I said, "I did not." Then the one CID man said, "This is a very nice apartment you all have here." I replied "Thank you." I said both my husband and I have very good jobs. My husband was now an E-4. Then one of the CID men said "Is there a storage space in the basement?" I said, "Yes?" They just knew they had me. They asked to see the basement and were shocked that there was nothing down in the basement which was our storage place. We had two ten- speed bikes because my husband and I rode a lot, and there were lots of boxes, each of which they checked. There were no cigarettes to be found. They thought they were going to find some cigarettes buried in the bottom of the boxes. I was so glad my mind led me right that time. They said again, "Mrs. Palmer, we think you got a call." I said, "No I haven't talked to my husband yet today," but I will call him and let him know about this." They said, all right. Then they left. All of the neighbors were outside standing around looking, hanging out of their doors and windows trying to listen, wondering what was going on. One of the neighbors next door came over and asked me if everything was Ok. If it had not been, what would they have done anyway? Not a thing, just wanted to be a curtain twitcher as well. The CID men came to our house at least once a week trying to make me confess about the ration cards. They had to have been out of their minds. They never did catch me with anything because after the first time, I stopped keeping my cigarettes at home. I never thought the CID was following me; my sick mind said, "If they were following me after I led them all around town, they would have gotten tired." But as I think about the situation, if they had of really wanted to bust me; I think they could have, but I do not know why they did not. I was very careful; I would ride around for hours sometimes if I thought someone was following me. I had given the black market game up because CID was watching me too closely and things got worse.

The Army was now messing with my husband in every way they could. One day Mike's captain told him that he had to take me back to the states; they gave him a month's leave to return me. I would not go, and Mike could not really make me because the government did not send for me. I went to Germany on my own, with my own money although the government was supporting me. It had gotten around the post that Palmer's wife was a menace to society. All the soldiers at the time were in the field but my husband did not have to go because he was supposed to have taken me back to the States. Then the soldiers returned from the field, and we were still there. Mike's captain asked him, "Did you get your wife back home?" Mike said, "No sir, she will not go."

Therefore, the Army had no other choice but to take things out on Mike. It was about a month before he had a hearing for not going to the field and not taking me back to the States, so they took all his rank. Therefore, he became a private once again. I felt it was my entire fault. I guess I took things for granted as I did many times. I did not know the unknown and at that time, I did not care. My husband felt he had to leave Germany because he had nothing. I had gotten a better job. I was working in the housing office in Hanau, Germany. I did typing and any other office duties that were asked of me. My salary doubled. I was making eighteen dollars an hour. I loved my job. There were a lot of people who were jealous of me, and I did not know why. I guess because I was making money, and I had skills to get a really good job, whereby they did not. Most of the ladies were just soldiers' wives. Everybody asked me how in the world I had gotten such a good job. At the time, I had two years of college and I graduated from computer school. I did have a little education behind me where the soldier's wives did not', all they did was have baby after baby. That was not my fault and was no reason to be jealous of another person. I could not even have a baby, I should have been jealous, and I was angry at times because I could not get pregnancy. Most of the wives had restaurant jobs which there is nothing wrong with that someone from Gilhousen where we lived where going to Hanau and saw me working in the housing office they went back and told CID. One day CID visited my boss he sent another co-worker to get me and my boss let me talk in his office. I had seen the man before when he came to my house looking for the rations cards. I said "are you people ever going to leave me along? I got a good job now and you are still messing with me." The CID man said Mrs. Palmer calm down. Mrs. Palmer he said "I have spoken to your boss and he spoke very highly of you". Mr. Rabbi your boss said "He picked your application over ten women; he felt you were one of the best qualified. "He said that is why you got the job. I said well "Thank you," the CID man said, "Mrs. Palmer you know you are a very intelligent woman. You can go fair in life, I do not think you really set your goal's high enough, I said, "Well who do you think you are coming over here to my job checking up on me, jeopardize my job, now I might get fired thanks to you, I do not need you telling me nothing about my life or what you think, I wish you go away and leave me alone." The CID man told me to calm down again; he went on to say, "The law wants you and your husband to leave Germany." I said to myself oh, "It is going to be some trouble now, I hear it coming. The military was going to force us to leave Germany by any means necessary. I told him to do what they do. He said they knew what I was doing but what CID wanted me to do was to be a snitch and tell on others who were black marketing. He knew I knew of some people who were selling to the Germans. I told him I would think about it. He went on to say if I help them out they would leave us alone, I would keep my job, and my husband would gain his strips back in a months' time. I told the CID man I would get back to him. He left me his card. He told me I had two days. He told me to go on back to work. I never heard any talk in the office from anyone about that situation, it was kept confidential. I was rather afraid because we had to live among the soldiers, and if I was to tell on them it maybe was a treat to get all of us who were Black marketing together at one time.

- I went home that evening and talked about the situation to Mike. I asked him what I should do. My husband said the decision was mine, and that whatever I choose to do, he would be behind me one hundred percent. I said, "But Mike, I cannot turn anybody in like that." I really do not want anyone doing me that way, and two wrongs do not make a right, although people have done me wrong and told on me. I should have thought of my husband and myself. We had to live with those people. I cannot be a snitch. Mike said "Jean, I respect your decision because if it were him, I would not tell either."

I never got back with CID. I continued going to work every day. I did my job. I was feeling very guilty as if everybody in the office knew. One day I went to my boss, Mr. Rabbi, and told him I needed to talk to him. He said, "Ok Doris, come on in my office." I talked to him about the day the CID man came to see me. I told him how embarrassed I was. He said, "No need to be no need to apologize." He assured me that no one knew about the situation but him, and he did not tell the others in the office. He said that was just my conscience working on me. The CID man never left me alone; I ended up quitting my job, and was hired at the post office in Frankfurt working third shift. That was the best shift to me because after we got finished with our work, unloading the trucks and waiting until a another truck came in we could sleep, we got up on the big stacks of mail that were bagged to go out to other parts of Germany. I learned how to pitch the mail as it were called; I also learned how to weigh the big boxes going to different parts of Germany. There were many soldiers working there which were their regular jobs.

I was really surprised because I thought all the soldiers had desk jobs or either they were guarding the tanks and stuff like that. My husband had a sit down desk job. There also were many civilians such as myself working at the post office. There were only two women working on the entire third shift and all the men were after us both, we both were married; but we had a lot of fun at work.

My co-worker, Tina, and I became good friends. There was this guy named John who was from the "Windy City," Chicago. He and I were good friends. John also became good friends with my husband, Mike. John used to say I was his girl because we had some good times at work, after work, and at our house.

I worked at the post office for about two months, and then Mike said it was time to go. He could not take the "Shit" from his superiors anymore; they were "Dogging him out" every day. They wanted us to leave Germany, so we made plans to leave. Mike said it would take him too long to get his strips back, and he probably would not get them back because his superiors would never allow that to happen. He was being punished for what I had done; really, we both did because I could not have done it without him.

I really did not want to leave Germany. My husband told his boss he wanted out. The army arranged for us to leave Germany; arrangements were made for the army to pick up our household goods to be shipped to the United States as well as our car. Our car was a dark apple red Jetta; there was no other car like it. Once it got to the States, everybody admired our car. It had a spoiler all around the car, the interior was like a black and grey tint, bucket seats, and it was a five speed. My husband had gone and got the car without asking me anything. I asked him why he got a five speed when he knew I could not drive it. He said because it was cheaper and he would teach me how to drive it. I did not want to learn at the time. I was upset of what he had done behind my back.

I continued to walk, or Mike would take me, or I would get a ride. Then I got tired of walking, not driving the car. The car was so pretty. Mike started me practicing changing the gears and getting used to the clutch while the car was sitting still for about a week. He showed me how to tell what gear I was in. There was like a wall when I moved the stick from side to side. That was my key to tell when the car was in neutral, and I took it from that point. The hard part to me was getting used to working both of my feet. I was scared of hills because I could not balance the car and would roll back. I used to go all around town in Germany to get where I was going. I used to avoid hills. After about a month I had the clutch down pretty good and was driving the car like a champion. Hills were no longer a problem for me. I learned how to balance the car using both feet. My husband was very proud of me that I learned so fast without stripping the gears.

From the time the paperwork went in, everything was arranged within the next ninety days for us to return to the United States. We had to pack up everything. The movers came and put everything onto the truck, and then we had to take the car to another part of Germany where the dock was at because the car had to be shipped. It was about a five- hour drive for ours friends to follow us there to drop the car off and bring us back. The car had to be inspected before leaving Germany. It was a new car, so we did not have any problems with that. We did not actually leave Germany until two months later. We had to give up our apartment and live in a guesthouse on post for those two months; the army did not pay for that. The expense got expensive. We had to eat on post or buy our meals because we had no way to cook. Those two months were a living hell, and we were ready to get it over. We had said good-bye to all of our friends we had made in Germany. The saying in Germany was that everyone would leave with one of three things. A baby, or a shrunk which was a big wall unit, or a cook-cook clock. We left Germany with a shrunk.

My 2 cousin and I at a family reunion.

CHAPTER EIGHT

Back To the States for Sister Wedding

O nce we got back to the States, I was supposed to be in my sister's wedding. We left Germany in June of 1990, and the wedding was September of that year. I had a little while to get prepared for the wedding. I was my sister's maid of honor, but before we had left Germany, I told my husband I would like to set up home in Atlanta, Georgia where my oldest sister Ola and my brother Sonny were. Atlanta is beautiful and it is steadily growing for Blacks. Mike, said, "Ok" because neither one of us wanted to live in Cleveland the rest of our lives. We had agreed we would stay in Cleveland until after the wedding. We got our household goods that took about two months to come. Everything happened around the same time: us getting the car, and our household goods. The wedding was over, so we could start trying to get our lives back together and find a place to stay.

My sister's wedding was the same color as mine, which was light blue. A week after the wedding I was ready to go on the Georgia and get set up. My sister was going to let us move in with her until we got on our feet, but Mike was not ready to leave Cleveland. I told him I was going if he wanted to or not. He could stay in Cleveland; he let me go on by myself. Mike let me take the car; I was upset because he had changed his mind, and I did not know why.

left to right
mother Chappell, mom and me

I found a job with a temporary services working in a candy factory. It was not the best job but it was work. I continued to ask the temporary office to find me something dealing with computers. About a month later, they had me a new assignment at an office named Standard Register. They told me that it was a very exclusive office and that I was to report to work business like. I wore a two- piece skirt suit and heels. I got to the building and it was very tall. As I walked into the lobby, it blew my mind. There was a big waterfall in the center of the lobby floor, lots of offices all around, and the cafeteria had a lot of trees. Also around it there were like palm trees and all kinds of plants. It was gorgeous. It took my breath away, and for me to be working in such a beautiful environment had never happened to me before. I was a very special lady. Once I got onto the elaborator and went up to my floor, which was the fifth floor where I would be working, there was plush carpet; it was very thick and pretty. There were all kinds of plants in the lobby. It was breathtaking also. I just could not believe that I was going to be working in that office. I was scared on the inside. I was on my best behavior. I even had my brief case; I was looking very professional. I went in and introduced myself. They were expecting me. Courtney was my boss, and she was Chris's secretary. Chris was the big boss. Everyone liked me from day one. They found out how crazy in love I was about computers. I did all of the data entry, updating, researched documents, checked revealed information, and printed all reports to be distributed to the proper office. Although I was only a temporary, I loved my job. The work was very challenging. I was in that position for eight months. The company had wanted to put me on the payroll as a full time permanent employee, but the corporate office in Dalton, Ohio, had a freeze on hiring any permanent people, so Chris gave me a big raise, and I stayed on with them. My husband stayed behind in Cleveland. He came to join me that Christmas of 1999. At the time, Greyhound was on strike, and it took him about a week to get to Atlanta. My sister who I was still living with agreed that he could join us until he got on his feet. When he finally got to Atlanta I picked him up from the bus station; he did not look like himself. He was very dirty and nasty looking. He told me if I had been on the bus for a week traveling, sleeping there, I would be dirty also. I overlooked it a little, but I did not know that Mike was strung out on drugs. At the time, I had no knowledge whatsoever about drugs. Mike and my brother, Sonny, were the best of friends, and I could not understand why. I knew my brother was up to no good. Mike would stay out all times of the night. Sometimes he would not come home for two or three days, hanging out with my brother until I started hanging over at the house a lot demanding to know what was going on. My husband really did not want to tell me what was going on. I was thinking that he and my brother were just getting "High." I had no idea crack would destroy a person's life. I had never been around that stuff before. Later on, Mike started stealing from my sister and I. He and my brother just disturbed my sister's little house. My sister was holding me responsible for Mike's actions; she wanted him to leave her house. He was my husband; he had no family in Atlanta. I could not just dump him like he was nothing to me. I was not ready to give up on him yet; I started looking for an apartment. I found a nice one. I saw in the newspaper where a special was running with no security deposit down. I took the apartment. We moved in the next two weeks. He was very happy of my actions. We ended up moving into an empty apartment. Our household goods were still in Cleveland. We arranged to go back to Cleveland to get our furniture. Meanwhile, I was glad about the apartment; it was nice. At least, I could cook again. My job gave me a week off to go to Cleveland to get our household goods and bring them back to Georgia. When we got to Cleveland, Mike disappeared. I had no idea where he was. I was so hurt, shamed, and embarrassed. He knew our purposes for going home, and he could not take the time to take care of our business. I sat around crying for days. I knew he had spent all the money he had. I did not want to tell my family, but I had to. I needed their help and support. My mother told me to go ahead without him. I did not want to leave him. He showed up after five days ready to go back to Georgia. I was so upset with him. He had rented for himself a black-on-black Cadillac, a brand new car riding around Cleveland as if he was a big man. All his family members were glad to see him because no one knew if he was hurt, dead, or alive. His family was saying stuff like, "Oh look at Mike." They were proud of the dumb stuff he had done. He had messed up the money he was supposed to get the truck with. My mother had to give me money to help us get back to Georgia.

I told Mike he did not give a damn about him or me. All he wanted to do was to show off, to make people think he was something he was not. He took the rented Cadillac back, and then we headed back to Georgia. Once we got back to Georgia, Mike worked with me to get our apartment fixed up; we did it in no time. We had bad but needed mattress. Within two weeks, I found some on sale. Mike never wanted to go with me to pick out a mattress, and I could not understand why, just being a lazy man, a guess. My uncle ended up taking me. I was thinking he had left that Crack- Cocaine alone because that is what he was telling me, but as everyone knows, people who are on that stuff are big liars. I am a living witness of that because I have had two brothers on it as well as myself. It kills and destroys lives. My husband and the neighbor down- stairs from us were very good friends. The neighbor was not his kind of people so I thought I could not see at first what they had in common. They were hanging together all the time. Time had told me they were getting high together. I got Mike a good job through the temporary service for which I was working. They fell in love with my husband because he was so good looking and had a very charming personality with the ladies. He got an outside job; he got in good with his boss who trusted him. Mike ran away with the man's truck for a few days. His boss called me. I could not tell the man anything because I did not know where he was. I told the man that when he returns, I would tell him to get in touch with his boss. His boss did not know he was on drugs and could not be trusted. When he did return, he told his boss all kinds of lies, and his boss fell for his shit and gave him another chance. He did well for a few weeks to build his boss's confidence back and then started his shit again. This time Mike stole all the man tools'; his boss wanted them returned, or he said he was going to press charges on him. Sure enough, Mike returned with more lies; I told him I did not want to hear it. His boss gave him chance after chance. I said his boss must really like him for his boss to keep on putting up with his mess or he was just ignorant to the fact of what people did when on drugs. Mike ended up leaving that job because he never gave his boss's tools back; he sold them.

Before my husband had first come to Atlanta, our brand new Jetta got stolen from right in front of my sister's house. She woke me up one morning very early because she was on her way to work; before I got up to get ready for work, she said, "Jean, where is your car." I said it is down there in front of the house at the bottom of the hill where I always park. She said, "No, it is not." There was a tree in the way whereby I could not see that well. When I opened up the front door and my car was gone, I started screaming and hollering at the top of my lungs. I could not believe the car was gone. My sister calmed me down enough to call the police; there was nothing else I could do. She asked me if I wanted her to stay with me. I told her, "No," to go on to work. I would be ok." I called my job and told them I would not be in because my car had been stolen. My job was sorry to hear that. After four days the police found my car stripped. As far as I was concerned, there was nothing left on the car; it looked so messed up to me. There was nothing left but the body almost. I mean the motor, transmission, and the seats were still there. I no longer wanted the car. I cried. I told my sister without insurance it would take me too much money to try and get it fixed back up. Once a car is stolen to me, it is never like it was in the beginning. I got it running, but it never was the same. I did not have the car in Atlanta a good month before the car got stolen. We had insurance while in Germany. The army told us that we had to pick up our own insurance again once back in the States. I kept putting it off. I was going to work every day paying all the bills. I even trusted Mike, so I gave him money to pay the phone, gas and rent. He brought receipts back showing me he had paid the bills. I felt good that he was doing things right and that at least he was trying, so I thought. He got over on me again, and again as well. He went somewhere and had the receipt stamped as if the bills had really been paid. Games drug addicts play-- they will come up with all kinds of lies. I know I told lies that were believable. Mike continued and continued to get worse. Mike's "get high" friend who lived downstairs from us with his wife and children did not really have anything in their house. The children were sleeping on old nasty mattresses. Both the husband and wife looked bad as that saying goes, "Who did it and what for." One day I came home from work and happened to see what I thought looked like my red television sitting in the front window in their living room. My mouth fell wide open in disbelief. I knocked on the door and the wife opened it. I looked at it and she said, "Oh, come on in." I said, "What are you all doing with my television?" She said I would have to take that up with my husband. I said, "I do not think so I want my television right now and I mean it." I told her if she did not give it to me that I was going upstairs and call the police. Then they will handle the situation. I knew it was mine because I had broken the antenna by mistake and had a hanger where the antenna goes. I told her whatever they had worked out with Mike; they take it up with him. They thought they had a television for a dime piece of crack. I did not want to know what they had worked out with him on that issue. I grabbed my television, unplugged it and went on upstairs. I was so upset with Mike, and I could not wait until he got home. When he did arrive home, he had nothing to say. I got to the point I did not trust him in the house alone. I did not trust him with money or anything else. I wanted to find out about this drug disease. I had started going to Alan-Non meetings. I found out that was his problem, and not mine. I had to set house rules and keep them enforced. Mike kept on telling me to learn how to deal with his disease to help him, but he did not even want to go to meetings. He would go in the front door and come out the back. It had gotten so bad I saw me hurting him, him hurting me, or him hurting himself; I did not want any of that to happen. He started selling my stuff out the house that I had worked so hard to get. I started looking for another apartment. I had gotten lucky. Across town from where we were living, I got the same deal which was no security deposit. The apartments were very old but very nice and clean. It even had a garbage disposal, two bedrooms, a big living room, and a big kitchen. I took the apartment. I gave them two months' rent in advance so I would not have to worry about paying rent for a while, I went back home like nothing had happened. Once I got my keys to the new apartment, I started moving boxes out little by little. Mike did not know what was going on at first until the apartment got so empty or his boy downstairs told him. After three weeks, he said "What is going on with you moving?" I said, "Now why would you say that? Of course I am not." He said, "Yea right." He was never home. He was too busy running after that white ghost to worry about if I was moving or not, and he could not stop me. I needed a car badly. My credit was so messed up until I could not get a car finance anywhere. I happen to be talking to one of the engineers I worked with, and he said, "Jean, I might be able to help you get a car." He asked me if I knew how to drive a five-speed stick shift car. I said, "Yes;" and he said I would need a thousand dollars, I told him, "No problem." A few days after that he brought the car to the job; it was so pretty. It was black with gray and black like specks seats. The car was a hatch back in which I fell in love with. He said, "Get in and drive it see how you like it." After driving the car, I had to have it. I told him to set up the deal. The car belonged to a college student who could not continue to make his payments. After the deal was made, I heard that we were not supposed to do that. I trusted him because he also worked in a law firm. He had some business partners that I had to meet. I did not know that it was not legit. I was scared; I asked my sister if she would go with me because she had a good head for business. We went and listened to what they had to say. I just was not going to give up a thousand dollars to get beaten. The student who the car belonged to was a law student his self. He wanted someone to take over the notes. That somebody was I. The guys were legit business men. My sister checked them out before I gave them a dime. I told him I will get back with him in a few days. He said, "Ok." After checking them out, my sister told me to go for the deal. She wanted to go with me to look at the big boss again who she fell in love with. He had the most beautifies green eyes you ever wanted to see. My sister asked me how well I knew the big boss who she was interested in. I told her I had just talked to him on the phone a few times, but the other guy I worked with. That is how I found out about the car. My sister wanted me to find out if he was married, and he was. I went in to get the paperwork started. I had to let my lawyer check the paperwork over before I gave them a dime. I took them the money. The car was mine, and I had a car note of $268.00 plus my insurance. I was happy and proud of myself. For the first time in my life, I got my very own new car, and it was black, shining like brand new money. I kept the car up. I added a pair of $600.00 black wheel. They were sharp. I had to make sure to get wheel locks. Everybody was looking at my car. I used to ram it up and fly like a bird in the air. A Black woman behind the wheel; I was getting a whole lot of play; it did make me feel good. I felt like somebody. I needed that because as soon as I got back home, all the dumb shit started. Mike knew I was getting the car, but he was too busy again to go with me and check the car out. After he saw the car, he fell in love with it. He thought he was going to be driving it, but I would not let him. I could not trust him. I was scared he would have given my car to the dope man for a few hits or something. I did break down and let him take me to work and pick me back up sometimes. Even then, he was late picking me up. He would take his dope friend all over town, and I stopped him from driving. I told him to go get a job and keep it.

I had everything planned to move into my new apartment. I let him keep the old apartment, which he tore up. He eventually got put out because he was not paying the rent. With my brother and uncle's help, I was able to pull the move off. They asked me if I was sure, Mike was not coming home. I said he has not been home in two days so why should he come now; and he had a warrant on him. His friend downstairs went and told him I was moving out, and he came home. I just knew he was going to start some trouble with me. He asked my brother and uncle if he could talk to me alone. I begged them not to leave me alone with him. They did anyway. They said, "Jean, you are his wife." I said, "I do not care. I never see him." It was on a Saturday morning. We got started at 8:00 a.m. We went to get the truck. My uncle went and got two friends of his to help. I had been taking little things over to the apartment three weeks prior to me moving in. I was planning for Mike to come home to an empty apartment. An hour before we got everything onto the truck, Mike popped up, storming into the house saying, "What the hell is going on, Jean." I said, "I am moving. I'm leaving you." he said, "Why? Why are you doing this to me? I said, "Like you do not know." My brother and uncle talked to him trying to calm him down because he was angry. I knew he was not going to try to do anything to me as long as they were there. Mike promised he was not going to jump on me. I did not trust him, and I was upset with my brother and uncle for leaving me alone with him. He could have killed me while they were outside sitting in the back of the truck. I left the window open so they could at least hear, and if anything happened, they could come running. I knew he was not going to do too much because he had a warrant on him for stealing his boss's tools. He kept on rising his voice at me, asking me why and please do not leave. I said, "It's too late. I have tried everything I knew and nothing worked. I am sorry, but I got to go now. If you need anything, I will still be around for you." I felt that way because he had no family down there. He asked me to at least leave him the floor model TV. I said, "Ok," just to keep him quiet. He would have sold it. I had already called the police on him because he wanted to tear up stuff around the house, and I was not going for that. When the police got there, he went down the back stairs and went in the back hallway to his friend house. I went out the front to talk to the police. I saw Mike looking out of the window. I did not want to tell on him; I just wanted my stuff out of the house and to go on my merry little way. The officer asked me where he had gone. I said I did not know. The officer stayed at the house until they got finished loading the truck. The officer informed me that if he did not want me to take the stuff out the house by law I could not. I said, "What." That was Georgia law. I was not going to tell Mike what the officer had said. After a week I went back to the old apartment to leave Mike food and money. There was nothing left in the apartment. I went into the back bathroom. There was a chair he had gotten from somewhere; there was a saucer, razor blade, and white stuff on the saucer. I said, "Oh my God." Mike has been up to no good. I left him some food and a few dollars knowing what he was going to do with the money. I went back the following week. When I stepped into the apartment, I could not believe my eyes. It was a real nice apartment when we moved in. My mouth dropped open, and tears started rolling down my face. He had taken the wall sockets out of the wall. All the light fixtures were gone, and in the kitchen, he had completely torn that up. There had been a build-in dish washier that he had taken out and sold for drugs. The stove and refrigerator were gone. I was surprised he had not pulled the carpet up off of the floor to sell that as well. He had hurt me so badly to see what he had done. At that time I really did not understand the disease at all. The apartment was in my name, and he was not on the lease. I had to paid that money back for the damage he had done to the apartment. The people in the office told me they saw him moving the stove, dishwasher, and the refrigerator out and put them onto a truck. I asked them why they did not call the police. They said because they knew he was my husband but I did not notify the office that I was moving because he would have had to go, and at the time I know he did not have anywhere to go. I had the property owner put a pad lock on the door. He started staying with some of his "get high" friends who had a house down the street so I was told, in a light blue house.

CHAPTER NINE

Husband Back To the States, Still Strung Out On Cocaine

I called my husband mother back in Cleveland and told her they had better send for Mike because there is nothing else I can do for him. He is homeless. He told his mother he was fine and he would let her know when he wanted her to send for him. I told her when that day comes to send him a ticket to get the ticket where he cannot cash it in. I finally went to the house where he was living. It was a beautiful house on the outside. However, inside the house there was nothing but pizza boxes everywhere. The people had lost the house and had to sell it. I told him he was going to get into trouble. The people who stayed in the house looked like they had not seen any water in months. That warrant stayed on him a long time until he made his mind up to go home. Until 2017 that warrant is still on him in Atlanta Georgia because he never answered to the charges for stealing his ex-boss tools.

Mike always wanted to know where my new place was. I would not tell him because all of the shit would have started all over again, and it hurt me to see him looking so badly. I kept on trying to get Mike to go back to Cleveland. He said he was going to get himself together and go to truck driver school. I told him I would help him because it was more to life than what he was doing. Mike told me he had started having bad dreams and seeing the devil. He drew a picture of the face he kept on seeing. The picture looked like the devil without horns or even a skeleton. It was enough to scare the living daylights out of me. Mike finally called his mother and said he was ready to come home. She sent him a one-way ticket that he could not cash in. I went to pick him up the night before and let him stay with me. We made love and I took him to the bus station that next morning. I told him I still love him because he was still my husband. I will always be there for him. That burden was off my heart now because I knew he was at home with his mother.

After six months, I was laid off from my sewing job. The company wanted to cut back; the first ones to go were the temporary people. I said, "Oh Lord, what am I going to do now?" I was paying my own way instead of living off of my sister. I got on unemployment right away. I had a little money saved up that would hold me for a while. The temporary service found me another job at Standard Register. It was a good- paying job, but they let me go after a year with the company. Until this day I never understood fully what had happened. My boss just told me it was a conflict among the girls. I did not fully understand what Chris was saying, but he said he had thought about the situation and he had to let me go, so I went back and talked to Courtney, the boss Chris's secretary, who popped pills and drank coffee all day. Everyone in the office knew not to step on Courtney's toes. That made me think she was making love to Chris. Courtney would not tell me anything; I knew; she knew. She acted as if she was scared of me all of a sudden. I knew that Courtney had brought her cousin into the company as another temporary worker to help me with the workload. During her first week in the office, she and I did not get along because she always wanted to make her Black jokes. I did not like it at all, and I let her know that. She was trying to tell me my job when I was supposed to train her. By her being Courtney's cousin, Chris was crazy about her as well. Rather she was right or wrong. She did not really know how to do anything. I did all the work. I was very upset behind Chris letting me go. However, I took it with a very good attitude. Chris even tried to get me placed in one of the other offices there in Atlanta as a full time permanent worker. He gave me the highest recommendation as he possibly could. Apparently, I was good enough to work in the office across town, but I was not good enough to stay there at the service office. I knew Courtney's cousin had something to do with it. I never found out the real reason. The other office Chris sent me to, was not hiring. I was out of a job; I could not find any kind of work. I could not pay my bills and keep my car note going. I did not want to ask my sister. I went to my church advisor at Saint Philips AME where I was a member. They provided help for some of my bills; that still was not enough so I started to give up slowly. I started doing slick things that I had no business doing to make money that I am not proud of today. I started using a system getting just about anything I wanted through the mail. I also stole credit cards from time to time. Clothes, furniture, household goods, and a lot more things were not a problem to get. I kept getting away with that. I stopped. I got tired and decided to make plans to go home to Cleveland.

I had packed everything up in my apartment my brother said he would drive me and my household goods to Cleveland, then take the truck back to Atlanta. Meanwhile, I was trying to sell some cordless telephones and a camcorder at the club. I met this man named Neal who was interested in the camcorder, but he did not have all of the money on him at the time. He gave me his telephone number and told me to call him the next day. I did call him; he wanted me to bring the camcorder to his house so he could check it out closer. I went to his house. It was ok. The house had potential; we talked about the camcorder and personnel things. He still did not have all the money. What I did not know at the time is that he was looking at me. He liked what he saw. He wanted to give me $200 in cash and $200 in cocaine. I really did not want the dope because at the time I was not using. I asked him if I brought his package back to him in a few days just like he gave it to me, could I get the rest of my money. He said, "Yeah." I left. I called him in a few days. He said if I still had the package, I could come get my money. I went right over to his house.

During that time we were talking on the phone back and forth.

I thought he was a sharp old man with class and finesse. He was a moneymaker; he sold drugs. He also did hair. I started liking him, but what I did not know is that he was interested in me the first time he laid his eyes on me. I took his dope back to him untouched. He was surprised, saying that the average person would have sold it or used it him or herself or even cooked it up. I told him I was not into all of that, and I did not know the first thing about the stuff. I had thought about selling it but to whom? He gave me my money with no problem. He said now that are business was over, I did not have to leave. I stayed and he cooked dinner for me.

As we were sitting at the table talking and drinking, there was a knock at the door. It was one of his old girlfriends who used to stop by from time-to-time to see what woman he had in his house. I did not know her. He opened the door and told her to come on in. He introduced us, but she was acting as if he was her man; she was saying things like she did not appreciate me being there and that she was still his woman. I then told him that I should go because she does not know me. He said at once, "No, you do not have to leave; I want you here." She said, "Well!" He told her she had to go, but she did not leave right away. She told him she wanted to talk. I went into his bedroom with his permission and sat on the bed to give them the privacy of talking. She did not really want to talk; she wanted to "Pick with me." She came into the bedroom and jumped onto the bed and kept on jumping. She was saying, "Yeah, this is still my bed." I said "Honey we are just friends; I just met him. I do not care about you. You are not going to sit here and mess with me." He walked into the room, and I said "I am out of here;" He grabbed me by my hand and said, "I will take care of this." I said that is what you said before. Now he put her out for real. That made me not want to deal with him at all. He kept on apologizing for her actions. "I said, Well she must really love you;" he said, "She had her chance," I gave her the world. I saw that he was a good man. At the time I did not exactly know what he did for a living. I saw that he really wanted me. So I started telling him about all my problems I was having. I also told him that Atlanta cost of living is very high and I could no longer afford to be there; therefore, I was going back home to Ohio. He did not want me to leave Atlanta. He told me he would help me out. I asked him why he would do that for a woman he does not know that well. He still said he would help me out until I got on my feet. He was going to pay the rent for my apartment. I had to leave because I was three months behind.

I had gone to court to buy some more time; my time had run out. I should have met him sooner. He and I started looking for another apartment for me. The ones that we looked at were very expensive, it was much more than I was paying. Although he said he would help me that just did not make any sense to me because why would I get something that was more than what I was paying. I told him I cannot and will not depend on a man for that because men always will let women down. I was not going to let him move me into a house or apartment that was $500 or $600 a month; I had a car note and insurance that I had to keep up. Time was running out. He suggested I move in with him. I think that is what he wanted all the time. I said, "Ok" because for real, I was not ready to leave Atlanta. I told him I had to change some things in his house before I came there to live. He said, "Ok". He also told me I could fix the house up any way I wanted to. There were these old curtains up at the windows that were nailed up; they had to go. He did not want anyone looking in his house. I told him I could not live like that. The bad part about the curtains was that they did not match. I told him I had to be able to look outside and let some sunshine in. He had a house full of furniture and so did I. His furniture was all old. My furniture was practically new; he wanted all my furniture in his house, and he was going to throw all his stuff away. I did not think that was a very smart move because if I ever wanted to leave him, it would have been just that much harder for me to get away and to get my stuff out of his house. He knew what he was doing. I was young. I had a floor model TV, washer, dryer, curtains, a couch bed, and a lot of clothes. My bed and a lot of other things I had to put into storage because there was no room in his house. I changed the curtains in the kitchen, living and dining rooms. Just adding a woman's touch made the house look so much better. I had to get two storage bins because what they had left was not big enough to hold all of my household goods. I did not

want to travel across town to look for a storage place. I got the largest
one they had, then a small one. Neal did not like me doing that at first;
he wanted more of my stuff in his house, but he got over it. There was
nowhere to put the washer and dryer; he paid someone to build me a
washroom on the side of his house. It was nice. He did not want me
going to the laundry mat.

I wanted to find work; at first he did not want me to work until I
started spending too much of his money. He was paying all of my bills
including my car note plus putting money into my pocket. I used to play
bingo a lot and go on bingo trips to different parts of Georgia, playing.
Usually on Sunday morning I was in church; my sister, Ola, and I sang
in the same choir; the church had six different choirs. It was a very big
congregation with five hundred members or better. We had a different
choir to sing every Sunday. My uncle was in the choir named Choir
Number One. They sang on the first Sunday. My sister and I were in
Choir Number Three we sang on the third Sunday; we were called the
Sanctuary Choir. There were the Gospel Choir, Men Choir, Teens'
Choir, and Children's choir. We were all good. I think the Sanctuary
Choir was the best that is why I joined them. Years later Sanctuary
Choir made a CD which I was not a part of, but my sister was. Every
year the choirs got together and put on a musical, "Toys for Tots," that
was some good music. The church would be packed; there was only
standing room. I could not get my man to ever go to church with me.
Everyone who was in our choir was between thirty and forty years of
age. We had two services, one at 7:00 a. m. and 11:00 a.m. which we
had to sing at both services. There is a message in gospel music, and
the words in songs motivate me to let me know to keep doing what I
am doing, especially if it is working.

A few favorite of my songs back then when I was in prison were
"Philips Hyman, "There's a Hero Lies In You," So Hold On; Earth-
Wind-and Fire, "Keep Your Head to the Sky, because master told me
one day I'll find peace in every way, and "We Have Come This Far by
Faith." I use to walk around and jog listening to my favored music. I
know He has never left me; I used to sing these songs all the time and
I still do till this day. Some people think I can really sing; I am ok. I

love singing for the Lord. For me I found out that my week always was better when I attended church.

I used to do stupid things to hurt myself like stealing when I really did not have to. I have always loved nice things. I did not mind working for them, but I had a mental misbalance that I never knew I had until I really got tired of getting in trouble over and over again. I could not keep a job for a long period of time. I thought that stuff was cute because I was doing something different so I thought. No one ever told me to stay on a job and retire. *"Nobody told Me That the Road Would Be Easy, and I don't Believe He Brought This Far To Leave Me."*

I learned how to do ceramics when I was in Germany; I got pretty good at it. When I was in Atlanta after my husband had gone back home to Cleveland; I told my man Neal, I wanted to make and sell my ceramics. He at first did not think I could do the work until he saw me. He did not have faith in me at first. He finally put me into a big shed in the backyard it was big enough for two cars to fit into. He helped me get all of my materials, and then he sent me home to visit my mother for a week. Went I got back to Atlanta, he had the shed put up; it was beautiful; he also built for me a work table; and there were two others long tables-- one to set my molds on after pouring and one to put the pieces on after opening the molds. Then the pieces had to be cleaned and sanded off. I had six shelves six feet tall with eight shelves on each; I had four of them on the back wall. The shelves were to stack and let my pieces dry. I ordered my kiln. There had to be a special socket for the kiln. I guess it was what you would call a 220 line. It took me time to learn how to work the kiln. The kiln would burn a lot of juice. It got three times as hot as a home oven did. There was a peak hole on top and two on the side. I stayed around the ceramic shop a lot and told them I was trying to learn how to cook my pieces; they taught me, plus I got books to read. I messed up at first, but I stayed with it and my work was beautiful. I started ordering my molds, things like kitchen objects, cookie jars, little what notes for the wall, Virgin Mary, Jesus, praying hands, the crosses, elephants, punch bowls sets and a lot of other things My brother used to help me sell my pieces. He was trying to get me to sell to big department stores, but I could not kick out a lot of pieces like that if I had big orders, so I thought. He got orders for me at bars that he knew the owners would like some of my pieces. I had a lot of personal friends and church members' orders'. I experimented with different kinds of paint to see what they could do. Once I got my workshop set up, it was very challenging work, learning and experiencing with the work. I did not know the reward was beautiful pieces that I did from the beginning to the end. My old man used to come home sometimes and say, "My God, Baby, you are mighty dusty." Sometimes I would devote ten to twelve hours a day in the backyard working on my pieces. I also had a room in the house where I cleaned and painted my pieces. I had to keep a supply of slip at all times to pour daily. Slip is like liquid clay. I poured every day because the molds could be used only once a day; then they had to be dried out. The flea market was about to open. It was not too far from where we were living. Frankie brought and had built me space enough for two booths which was too much space. I rented one side out to an African lady. She started not wanting to pay the rent for selling her African clothes in one of my spaces.

People did not want to pay me what my pieces were worth. My man got me business cards printed up. I was the owner, seller, and an entrepreneur. I started getting with other people who were doing the same things as I; and I stated giving a lot of shows. My best seller was my elephants and this stature of a naked man and woman. I had this unicorn that I loved. Those items were very popular. I started selling at parks, colleges, and different functions that came up. My man was a great inspiration to me; without his help my ceramics business would have never gotten off the ground.

Things started changing with my man; all of a sudden he wanted me to work. I guess I was getting too expensive for him. He started cracking on me in front of his friends that I did not know how to do anything. I told him he was the one who did not know how to do anything but sell drugs. I also told him I had a little education. I have always had good jobs. I went out and got a job so I did not have to hear his mouth. It was a telemarking job; I was selling vacation homes, and I did pretty well at it. I worked only part time, but the pay was hourly plus commission. I had to start paying some of my own bills. After a while, the devil got into me.

My business partner had not paid me rent in two months; she always had some reason why she did not want to pay her part of the rent. Then, I stole one of her checks and made it out for $200.00. It was not that I needed the money; it was the principle behind the situation; she thought she was being slick. By us being business partners, we had papers drawn up whereby we gave each other consent to use each other's signature. She really could not do anything about it. It took a while for the check to return. She had no idea it was me. She was telling me about it and thought it was her boyfriend who had gotten a hold of her check book.

My man Neal could not stand the heat due to him being a big drug dealer. Those African people came looking for me in truckloads. They knew he knew where I was, but he did not tell them. They wanted to kill me because there was nothing legal she could do to me. Since she could not send me to jail, she sent her people after me. My man put me up in a hotel. He also tried to pay double the face value of the check, but they would not take the money he had so much dope, more than I had ever seen before. I know why they call it "Dope"-- because it is for "Dopes. "People need to wake up and realizes that it is killing them. I can talk because I have been there and done that over and over again until I finally got it right and made up in my mind to let go and let God direct me. It worked. My man used to tell me how his last woman used to take his dope and sell it for herself. I cannot talk because that is what I was doing as well. He also sold weed. I was selling dime bags. People started wanting weight. I could not steal that much without him really missing it.

Then I went back to smoking dope because my man used to let a women come to the house and smoke, so I joined them. At that time I stayed home and got "High". My man kept on telling me, that I was getting worse smoking that stuff. I said, "No", I'm not." He said, "Yes, you are, I have been watching you." I would smoke only once a week at that time. I was still working on my ceramics, going to work every day, played bingo, and worked my business at the flea market. I did not have to go anywhere for dope because all I wanted was right there in the house for me. I did not see where I was so bad and I did not lose any weight. A matter of fact, I wish I had because I was too hippie. My man used to tell me all the time, "Baby, you are fine the way you are".

I feel today that if a person do wrong in life, God will get him/her. My mother used to tell me that all the time, "God do not like it when a person does wrong, and you will get paid back, and it will happen before you leave this earth." Sometimes when a person does wrong in life, the devil gets behinds him/her and steps in and hits that person at the lowest point in his or her life. That is what happened to me. The devil's job is to kill, steal, and destroy your life in one way or the other.

I had to leave Atlanta, Georgia because my man thought that was best for the both of us. I did not want to leave, so I kept on telling him to fix it. He said he could but that it would take time and he did not know how much time. I wanted to face my partner in court. There was no way I would have lost. My man said they would have hunted me down. After the judge saw the agreement she and I had and the documents that I had on her, I think I would have won the case. We went to court and I did win. She was so angry, two weeks later she said that I broke into her house and robbed her at gun point. My man knew that was a lie; however, I had no way of proving that. I could not take the chance of going to jail. That is what brought me back home to Cleveland.

I had to leave all my things behind; the flea market went unattended, and my man did what he could. My furniture that was in storage, my workshop, and my furniture I had in my man's house, he took care of it for me. He closed the flea market and kept paying my storage. I packed the car with as much as I could and drove on back to Cleveland by myself. I had made that drive before by myself, but this time the car was full. I drove until I got tired; then I stopped off at Cincinnati where I have an uncle and cousins. I stayed overnight with them; therefore, it took me almost two days to get home.

As I was doing slick stuff, it took a while to accomplish things in life, but all it took me was a blink of an eye for God; to take it all away to start over again only because the lesson God wanted me to learn was not learned. I was not living for God; I was blind and I could not see.

I thought I got myself together, but I could not understand why I was having so much bad luck; nothing was going right for me. Everything was wrong. I would get to a certain point in my life, then fall right back down a little farther. I always sprung back up every time, but I felt it was coming to a time in my life where I was going to hit rock bottom, and I would stay there in my life if I did not change. I had a lot of guilt feelings, that I hated but I just kept continuing to do the things I was doing one thing for sure everybody that knew me, knew if nothing else, I was going to keep me a job regardless what else I might have gotten myself into. One thing is for sure it is so easy to get into trouble but so hard to get out of it. I did not understand *consequence neither did I care at the time.* I made a lot of amends to family members and others I had hurt or wronged because that is what the program of alcohol anonymous told me I had to do. Some people accepted my apology and others did not and that was and is ok because the only one I can change is me.

My great grandmother

From left to right: My two sisters Teressa, Ola, and I

CHAPTER TEN

Back to Cleveland and On the Road with a trucker

When I first got back to Cleveland, I had made plans to live with an old girlfriend of mine and her husband. They said they would be more than happy to have me. After two weeks of being home, I had found a little job with a catalog telemarking Service Company. I did not like the job too much. It was too much of a script to read. The company wanted the script read just as it was. Larry Gains, Diane's husband, said that I had a drinking problem. I really did not. I just took a drink or two every day to ease my nerves. Larry started hiding the liquor from me; he said I was drinking them out of house and home. At times, I brought my own and offered some to them. My husband and Larry Gains were best of friends. My husband was on drugs and Larry did not want him around so I promise the Gains I would not tell him where I was living. That did not work out too long because I did not like their style of living.

I ended up moving back in with my mother because I could have gotten along better with my mother than with Larry Gains. My main priority was to get myself together and find me a job and get me a place to live. During the time I moved in with my mother, I got a job working with my nephew at Delcom doing over the phone sales for the *Plain Dealer*. It was only party-time but full time money. The opportunity was there to make a lot of money. I got paid hourly plus commission. I did very well. If we made more than fifty sales in a week, our name went up on the board. I wanted to be up on the board every week but it was hard. It caused for a lot of dedicated work and took me a while to do it. Once fifty sales were hit, the money started. I was one of the top salespeople alone with my nephew. I came from Georgia with $2,000. I knew I was going to need that money to live on and pay my car note.

I went back to Atlanta to get my furniture after being home for 6 months. Once in Atlanta I called my ex-man and told him I was in town; he did not want me to come to the house. I loved that pop up call. He told me he had company. I told him I did not care. I told him I had been on the road all night and I'm tired and I would like to take a bath. I went on to the house, he let me in. I got in the house and found this woman on my bed couch, asleep with no sheets on the bed. He knew I was going to get upset about that. He should have not had her in his bedroom. I said, "I will be dog gone," and then steps another woman coming out of his bedroom. I said, "Oh man, you must have had an orgies last night or something," but I had promised him I would not get angry. All I wanted to do was to take me a bath and change clothes. He offered me a drink, and I took it. Both the women in his house looked to be hung over from the night before. One of them cooked breakfast, I was still angry about him letting one of the women sleep on my couch bed without a sheet. I did not eat breakfast; she might have put something in it. He had promise to take care of my things. Then I left and went over to my sister's house. I told him to call me when his company left and I'll come back. He knew I was coming in town; I should have never walked into those women. To me he showed me that he did not care. He begged me not to leave and go to my sister's house, I told him he should have never had them there, and he had to take them home. I was not going to sit around his house and look at that mess. The ladies were trying to talk to me, asking how my trip was. I said, "Long, very long." They introduced them- selves to me but

I did not have much to say. I just figured they were two hoe's trying to get some money out of him. He called me at my sister's house after he took those two women home; I went back to his house. He was telling me how much he had missed me and how much he had cried when I first left Georgia. He said he had never cried over a woman before like he had done for me because I was out of his life. He was really torn up inside I had thought. He said he loved my little nasty drawers. He also said I had thrown away everything we had worked so hard for. He was planning to marry me and pay for my divorce from Mike; I was too wild back them, and I did not know who I was. We talked and talked; he finally went and got the truck for me, but he did not want me to take my furniture out of his house. I told him it is mine, and I had found a very nice two-family house for only 285 a month. I was renting the upstairs, I also had the attic and basement which the basement was a good place to put my washer and dryer. My brother and uncle loaded the truck from two storages bends for me. My man Neal did not want to help with the loading. My ex-man wanted to keep my washer, dryer and floor model TV, my shed that was in his back yard, there was no way I was getting that down. It took the men two weeks to put it up. He told me to take that as well. He was being funny because he was angry that I was taking all my things out of his house. I told my brother I would pay him to drive the truck to Cleveland, and he did. We got a car dolly to pull my car on the back of the truck so I could ride with my brother in the truck. The car and the truck were packed.

My brother knew I had a little money to live with. Once back in Cleveland, he tried to get every penny he could and then some. My brother wanted to charge me a 1,000 to take me to Cleveland and take the truck back to Georgia. I told him that was too much. He said, "Anybody else would of charge you a lot more." Probably so, but he was not *anybody,* he was my brother, and I told him he should have been ashamed of himself for being money hungry. He did help me a lot. I would not have had anyone else to do that for me.

He stayed home a week. My mother was glad to see him. Once in Cleveland he helped me unload the truck and put the things into my new place. My brother and I were the closest out of the six children. In high school everyone thought we were twins. I never thought we looked that much alike, but people said we did.

As time went on, I ended up meeting this truck driver but he was talking to this woman my friend knew. She was not treating him right, and I took him. He stayed on the road, and he was good to me. He wanted to spend a lot of time with me; therefore he made sure his company did not send him too far that he could not get back to Cleveland within a few days or so. His runs were like to Detroit, Chicago, Akron, and surrounding areas. Every time I looked up he was home. I was glade about that because he showed me that he cared. At times he was gone for a few weeks or so. Still, he made sure that I was taken care of.

He asked me to go on the road with him. I said "Yes" because the truck always fascinated me. Riding in one just turned me on. I told him I hoped we could go to California because I had an aunt and cousins out there that I had not seen in over ten years. Aunt Fannie is one of my mother's younger sisters. She is also the lightest of my nine aunts and uncles. He really did not want to get a load out West because he said he could never get back North. I put up a big fuss until he went ahead and pleased me. We went to Reno Nevada that was a lot of fun playing the slot machines. I hit on the quarter machine. Lights started flashing, bells started ringing, and I started hollering "Oh my God." I was grabbing the quarters. I asked him to go get me something to put the quarters into. That was my first time out west, and I always have liked to travel. The furthest we went was to Stockton, California. Once we got there, I called my Aunt Fannie; she lived in Los Angeles. She said I was still five hours from her. I was so disappointed; there was no way we could have gone five hours out of the way with the trailer. I just talked to her on the telephone for about an hour. At every truck stop we stopped at, there were hoes everywhere trying to make a dollar. One night we were in the back of the truck asleep. There was a knock on the truck door. It woke me up I told Jo "Somebody is knocking." He said, "See who it is;" I climbed up front and looked out. The woman had climbed onto the truck. When she saw me, she started apologizing. I said, "What are you selling?" Then I said he does not want any; he's has it all right here. I started laughing. Jo said, "Jean, you are crazy." I was only having fun because after two week on the road, I was ready to go home. I got tired of eating junk food; I got tired of eating on the road, bouncing up and down in the truck started getting to me. I had to make the trip enjoyable, one time we were traveling and the breaks started to smoke real badly; we were going down Mt. Evert. I was so scared when he stopped the truck; I got out and said, "We could have got killed." I told him "I will see you at the bottom of the hill." A greyhound bus came by, and I put my thumb out, I was trying to hitch-hike a ride, the diver did not pick me up. I was forced back into the truck. He was caring frozen chicken; that was a lot of weight behind us; as soon as possible he had his breaks checked. There were a lot of accidents on the road maybe because it was winter. There were cars and trucks turned over in the ravine. Traffic was backed up for hours. He got out the truck to see what was going on and how long we would be sitting still like that. He came back to the truck. At first I would not let him in. He said, "Jean, stop playing; open the door, It is cold out here. I laughed and opened the door. I had to do things like playing those games with him whenever I could because I had gotten bored and tired of the road. We were sleeping in the truck except that one night; his company put him up in a hotel for a night until his clutch was fixed the next day. I was in a real bed; that was something I had not seen in a month. He was trying to make the trips enjoyable for me. I had gotten tired of playing cards. Once we got out of Stockton California, it was just like he had said; he could not get back north. One of the deliveries to Stockton was frozen food he had to drop off, and unload the truck himself, and had to take the skids and put them onto the dock. Then he had to put this plastic wrap around the skids. I wanted to help him to have something to do, but he would not let me; he said that was not for a lady to do. There were a lot of men on the dock, and other truck drivers making deliveries. He did not want them looking at me. There were a lot of good-looking men standing around the dock that I did talk to. He was watching me too closely where I could not even get a phone number. I had on a pair of tight blue jeans shorts and a matching tee shirt. He kept telling me to stay in the truck but I did not listen. I told him that is all I do is stay in the truck. "I want some kind of excitement other than looking at you."

While in Stockton; we saw a gang fight. We had stopped at a corner store to ask where we could find the liquor store. As we were going back to the truck, across the street was a group of young people who we did not pay any attention to. This one girl came running across the street where we were and hit this one girl dead in the mouth. I said, "Did you see that?" He said, "Yell," come on and get in the truck because it is going to be some shit," and sure enough, the rest of the young people went running across the street to join her. A fight broke out. I'm not sure if it was a gang fight or not. We were watching from the truck. This all happened in the ghetto. They did not have any guns, sticks, chains or knives that I saw. The fight looked to be fair. One girl got her top torn off, and she had very large tits that were flopping everywhere. However, we finally found a liquor store, and ordered us a pizza. We had stopped for the night. We had one more load the next morning in Nevada to drop of some tires. Then his company promised they would give him a load going back to the north. We were late getting to the place to unload. The company had given his north load to another driver. We were pulling in, and the north load was pulling out. I wanted to cry because now I did not get to head back home. Joe had to stay on top of his company to get a load heading back north.

Now I had started to feel nasty and dirty. There were times I had to use the bathroom so often; Joe did not want to stop; I started peeing in a cup and throwing it out of the window. I even started to smell like urine. They were giving him loads back and forth to other parts of California and Nevada. We finally were heading back north with loads on the way, I thought. I woke up one morning and asked him where we were, and he said the company had given him a load to Reno. I said, "Oh no." We were supposed to be going home. I knew he had no control over the matter because if he had, he would have had me home weeks ago. We were half way home and turned around in the opposite direction. We went back to where we had come from.

I could not believe that was really happening. He tried to worn me in the beginning of how hard it would be to get back north. I said "As long as I live I will never get on the road in a truck again." He told me to calm down and that was my pay back for locking him out of the truck. I reached over at him and started to hit him with my hat. He knew how badly I wanted to go home.

Once we got back to Cleveland, he had his whole family laughing at me about how I was acting when we were on the road. I was nothing compared to when he took his cousin on the road with him. He had his cousin on the road for a week. His cousin got drunk and said he was going to take a walk to check out the truck stop and the surrounding area. He wondered off somewhere and fell down into a ravine. He had to dig and scratch into the dirt his way out to the top of the ravine Joe said "All you could see was his hand and foot prints alone with his very swollen face looking like somebody had "kicked his butt."

CHAPTER ELEVEN

Trouble between Two Men, Husband Gets a Good Job

My husband had tried to convince me that he had changed, and we should try to act like a family again. He and I were not together at the time. I gave him another chance. Before I could tell Joe what I had done, he came into town because something had happened to his truck, and he did not let me know he was coming to my house. I was not home. Mike was at my house. Joe had gotten word to me to pick him up at the bus station at 10:30 that morning. I had a test to take that morning at 8:00. I was hoping I would have been finished in time to pick him up because I was right downtown, but I did not finished with my test in time. I got finished with the test at 10:00 a.m. and shot to the bus station, but his bus had come in early, and he was gone. I said, "Oh lord; there's going to be some mess now." I panicked. I called home immediately and told Mike to put the double lock on the door. He asked why "ám I was expecting trouble." I told him Joe was in town, he has the house key. As long as the double lock is on the door he can't get in and he would probably wait on the porch until I get there or he will leave. I asked Mike to please do not start any trouble he promised me he would be nice. By the time I got home, everything looked pretty calm. Before I could get out of the car, the lady downstairs stopped me and said there were all kinds of police around the house pulling guns on Joe talking about he did not live there and he had a gun. The lady stated she did not know my husband. She knew Joe and she knew that he did not live there. I felt so badly that Mike told that lie about Joe having a gun.

I went upstairs to talk to Mike. He said that Joe was trying to get into the house; Mike went to the porch and told him that Jean is not home. He asked him what he was doing in the house. Mike told him that he was my husband. Mike said that Joe "Was acting as if he wanted to kick the door in. Mike said he warned him not to do that. However, Joe would not stop, so Mike called the police and said there was this man with a gun. When the police got to the house they got out of the cars pumping their shot guns straight at Joe and told him to put his hands up. He was shacking and did not know what was going on or what to expect. They shouted to him where is the gun. Joe said, "What gun; I do not have a gun. What are you all talking about?" The police told him to keep his hands up and not to move. After the police searched him and did not find a gun, they started talking to him. The lady downstairs from me had told the police he could stay there in her house until I got home. He was made to leave.

When I finally got home, Joe asked me why I did not tell him. I told him I did not have time; He said he had paid a man to bring him to the house. I felt so badly. I was so upset with Mike and I told him he did not have to call the police and lie. Mike felt I was sticking up for Joe. A few days after all that had happened, things were back to normal. Joe had gotten all of his things out my house and told me he would not be any trouble to me, but if I ever needed him, he would be there for me. He said he would always be my friend.

My husband had gotten lucky and got him a job at Greyhound bus station making good money. I was thinking that maybe we would have gotten things together and grow old in life so I thought. I thought he had left that crack alone. He did well for the first month; then he started missing work, lying about when he got paid. He said the company kept his check due to him paying out child support; he was lying because he did not prove it. He just talked it, and by this time, I did not believe anything he said he was telling lie after lie. He was not paying any bills; he had the rent two months behind. One time he took my car and was gone for two days. He did not care that I had to go to work. That crack was calling him. I told him he had to get out of my house because I could do badly all by myself. He moved back in with his mother. I was going there to see him and his mother from time- to- time.

One of his trips was to Chicago where he met this light-skinned ticket agent, and he brought her and her two babies to Cleveland. I said, "Oh boy, here comes some more mess." Mike's new woman did not know anything about him. Other than he was a good- looking man who was a playboy. I had found out he made plans for this woman and her two babies to come to Cleveland for a few weeks. That was a big laugh. I said, "She is a fool; his sex was not that good." I used to take his mail down to his job. I asked him how in the world he could take care of her and her two babies when he could not take care of me. I knew that relationship was not going to last. He had a daughter of his own he was not doing anything for. His daughter was crazy about her daddy. She looked up to him. He started trying to dog me out in front of this new lady from Chicago. I told her "It is just a matter of time before he dumped you." I also told her that she will find out about how he was; I laugh and walked away. She just looked at me. I told Mike "I bet you do not keep that job a year." and he did not. I stopped all commutation with him.

One of Mike's brothers and I were very close. I use to go on his job from time to time to ask how Mike was; I knew he was going to tell me the truth about the lady from Chicago and her babies. My brother-in-law told me he hated that woman because she was lazy; her babies tore the house up and she lets them. All her and Mike did was stay in the bedroom, expecting someone else to take care of her children. Maybe they both were getting high. I said they are really in love right now. He told me that she was going on his routes with him, leaving the babies at home for his mother to take care of. After a while, Mommy Palmer got tired of that mess and told them they had to take the babies with them. Mike was too sorry to get a place of his own for him and his new family.

Mike was still using drugs big time. His brother told me he had been in the hospital; I said what for? He said one day him and his woman went to the store to get some fish. Mike send her in one store and told her he was going to get something else from another store across the street; when she came out the store with the fish he was gone, he was nowhere to be found. He pulled one of his fast numbers on her, he was up to his old behavior again, and it was funny to me. She looked and looked all over the area for him. She went on back to the house with the fish and told the family what he had done. He was gone for two days. They got a call saying he was in the hospital which he had made up something for them to keep him or he hit the pipe to hard and thought he was going to die; he had already had high blood, and he had a pin hole in his heart. He was on a lot of medication. He had no business messing with the pipe.

Four months later, I ran into one of his cousins at the shopping mall. She asked me how he lost that good job at Greyhound. I had no knowledge of him losing his job. I had not seen him or heard from him in months. He had a new woman and did not have time for anyone. It was as if he and I were not married. I knew things were going to go downhill for him because he was not about the right things; he was thinking he had something going on.

Mike and I got "*high*" together one time. He had stolen dope from me. He was cheating on me and he thought I was so dumb that I did not know what he was doing. One day I was downtown Cleveland at the license bureau trying to get my plates. He knew my car from a mile away I was looking for a parking space and decided to go ahead in the parking lot. As I pulled in, there was this man standing at a distance from me smiling. As I got out the car I got close to him and I realize it was Mike my husband. We were separated but still married. My mouth fell wide open. It was Mike the first thing I asked him was where his new lady was. He said, "She went back to Chicago." I told him I was sorry to hear that, but I knew that was going to happen. I also told him that while she was in Cleveland he did not know who I was." I asked him "Why should I have time for you now?" He said because he was my husband. I said, "Not anymore, remember that." Those were his words. He let out a small laugh. He waited on me until I got finished with my business. He was always a charmer, but that no longer worked with me. I knew he wanted something, but I just could not go back to him again, not after the mess he kept on doing to me. Since he was on the bus, I offered him a ride.

I had a pocket full of money so I took him to have a drink. I told him he was never going to have any luck if he did not change; I guess he never believed me. I know today he wishes he had of listen and stayed with me. I told him that he and I would not work anymore. There had been too much hurt and pain, and I took him back repeatedly, but he kept doing the same thing. We could be friends and nothing else, and we were. He never stopped smoking crack. From time-to-time, he used to call me. I had got tired of him.

I met another man named Levi whose brother I worked with who name was William. He used to talk about his brother all the time. He said his family had to ride to Grafton to get Levi; I should have been scared of him knowing he was just getting out of prison. It seemed like that was the kind of guys I was attracted to; for whatever reason, I do not understand it today, knowing I am better than that. He had done four and a half years in prison. His brother William use to tell him how nice of a women I was, and who was built up like a "Brick house." I did not know my worth back then, and I wished I had.

After meeting him, I said, "He wants some of my loving, and every woman looks good to him about now, just getting out of prison." I know he was very horny. He had not had a woman while he was locked up. I was convinced to meet him. His brother-in-law picked William and I up from work that night and Levi was in the car. I was on the bus at the time since my car was in the shop. They were in a white Cadillac; I got in the front seat. I was supposed to be impressed by the car and I was; but it was not Levi or William's car. It was in the wintertime, and I had gotten into an accident on the bus; I was going home from work one night. I had a neck brace on; I was wearing a yellow leather coat with a fur hood, jeans and a sweatshirt. We went over to William's house. We had very little conversation on the way but William kept picking with Levi, saying what wrong man, the cat got your tongue? You have not even said anything to Doris. I laughed because William was a fun man. Levi just kept looking at me, trying not to let me see him looking. Once we got to the house, his brother fixed us a few drinks. Then Levi started talking a little. I really was surprised that Levi did not ask to make love to me; he did not even ask for a kiss. I was glad that Levi's mother who he was living with did not live too far from me. Before he took me home, he wanted me to meet his mother. That was unusual for me because most men do not want to take a woman who he has just met, home to meet mom. We stopped at his house; his mother seemed to be a very nice little old woman. I came to find out that his older brother had been one of my teachers in high school. Mr. Davis was his name. Levi and I were in the basement, and he did kiss me and said, "Doris, I really do like you; you are very pretty." His talking did not go to my head because really at the time, I did not think I was pretty at all. I never got the big head when people gave me a compliment. I heard that all the time, but I did not believe it.

my dog Terri and me at mom house

At the time I had my Terri who was my dog which my baby sister and her husband gave to me because she started having too many children. They did not want the dog around the baby, and they no longer wanted to take care of the puppy. The dog and I were best friends, Terri was a full bread Boston terrier. I called her my baby because when I first got her, she could not walk upstairs, and she was stinking very badly until I had to go to the drug store to buy items to bathe her in.

After being dropped off that evening, I went on upstairs to feed Terri. She was glad to see me because I had been gone from her all day. I always had to lock her in the kitchen because I did not want her all over the house when I was not at home. I always let her out so she could run around. She was house trained, and I did not have any trouble from her except at first. She was telling me where she wanted her bathroom to be because every time I put paper in one spot, she would not use it. So I started putting the paper where she was using the bathroom at and I did not have any other trouble out of her. She hated to go outside in the winter. I took her on walks and took her to the park. I also let her on the porch because I lived on the second floor. She used to run so fast through the house until I could not keep my rugs straight because she messed them up. I used to think she was going to kill herself running so fast. I was smoking crack them. As soon as I feed her, I would feed myself by putting me a rock into my pipe to smoke. I put a whole twenty piece into my pipe, and I would be in heaven so I thought. Then I would say to myself, "Man that shit is good." I was around the house by myself, tripping on my dog and myself. At times Terri would get on my nerves; she acted as if she knew I was getting "High," so I would lock her in the kitchen where she could not see me. Levi knew I liked smoking rock cocaine, and he said he would never mess with another woman who smokes. What I did not know about him is that he was a con man. He had said he would have never known I was smoking because I keep a nice clean house, and I worked every day. I was in my early stages of my addiction and believe me, it slowly took me down. I ended up catching another case because I could not stop smoking that mess. I got put on three years' probation. I said I could do that because I did not get into a lot of trouble; however, I was dealing with a no good man. He found out

I was on probation. I had to have my urine tested once a week. . I just could not understand why he did me the way he did. He started buying three and four hundred dollars' worth of cocaine a week. Therefore, I had started smoking more because he fed it to me, and I was too dumb to say "No". I trusted him, and he was no earthly good. He wanted to see me strung out on the mess. We both were smoking, and I was still going to work every day. I started trusting him, and that was a very wrong move. I gave him a key to my house; he was at my house when I was at work. I did not know he shot-up dope. I used to wonder and ask him all the time why he sweated so badly, he also liked-Irish Rose wine. I used to drink it as well. I never broke out in a cold sweat as he did. He used to nod off all the time. I said, "Man, what is wrong with you?" He made up some old lie. I just used to watch him. I started getting a little weary of him and I started to distrust him. My brand new type- writer came up missing that he knew nothing about. He said he had not seen it. I knew that was a lie. He told me while I was at work; he had some of his friends over. That red flag went up. I talked about things and then let it go. He and his friends were stealing from me, and I allowed it, like a fool. He kept telling me he was going to get my typewriter back. That was a lie; he was just bad news all around. I told him that I did not want anyone in my house when I was not at home. He broke into the lady's house downstairs and turned her bedroom upside down and found three hundred dollars. She was really upset, and she knew he had done it. She told me that I kept bad company. No one could prove he had done that.

I have always been a nice dresser; I have nice clothes, shoes, hats, purses and coats until it was so hard for me to keep up with all of my things. I loved my blue fox jacket that had come from Germany. I know that no one took it but Levi. He was a con-man, and he did a good job conning people. I used to put my fur in storage every year to get it treated to keep it looking good; if I had of done that that year, I would still have my coat. When a person is living in the fast lane as I was, negative things like that are bound to happen. I have seen it happen to the best of people.

Left to right: Dad, me and mom

My brother Michael and I

CHAPTER TWELVE

Part one: Prison life Again and That environment Of Doing Three Years

One day my probation officer (p.o) had told me my judge wanted to see me because I came up with three dirty urines. I jumped out of the chair and said there is no way; I have not been using any drugs. She was convinced and she was on my side. She set the court date for me. I was scared and wondered how in the world I got three-dirty-urines when I was not smoking that much. A few days later I got a secret indictment for me to go to court about passing bad checks. There came double trouble. If it all was the same case, I had not passed any other bad checks so the case was given back to my original judge who I was on probation with. Levi knew what he was doing, pumping me with all the dope as he was; he knew I would not pass a drug test because it took too long to get out of the system. What I did not know was the more a person smoked, the longer it took to get the drug out of the system. Three days to get clean did not always work. I learned the hard way on life. Levi wanted me to go back to the penitentiary; he did not give me any moral support; when my real sentencing came around, he was nowhere to be found. After I had the three dirty urines, he called my p.o and said that I was going to get someone to drop urine for me because I was scared, and if I was dirty all those times, I probably was still dirty, he told me that was a good idea, but. I could not find anyone to do that for me. I lied and told him it was all set up for someone to drop for me. I got home that evening and he asked me if it had worked. I said, "Yes, we got away with it." I went to see her that next week, I sat down and said, "How are you today?" like I usually asked her. She said immediately, "Oh Doris, I heard you had someone go drop your urine for you." I stood up and went off. I said, "That's a lie. I know nobody called you but Levi Davis;" she said she could not tell me that. I told her she did not have to. He was the only person I told that too. I have never had anyone drop my urine for me. I was very upset by his action. What did I expect--he was a con man and a no good one at that.

My probation officer told me she had talked to a police officer about my case and said he said the judge probably would leave me on probation and let me go to a rehab center. My p.o and, lawyer had worked very hard trying to get me into a rehabilitation center, by the time I went back to court, which was July 22, 1992. I was to start at the rehab facility on July 28th. I was working from 3:00 p.m. to 8:30 p.m. I was glad they found a rehab in which I could go to. It would have been outpatient from 9:00 a.m. to noon Monday through Friday; that way I could still keep my job. A week before I went to court I met this guy in the bar downtown in Tower City in Cleveland, Ohio. I had gone there to meet this very old friend of mine. While waiting for him to arrive, a guy next to me saw I was sitting by myself. He started a conversation with me. He was not a very handsome man but he was not ugly either; he was rather on the heavy side and very tall. He knew how to treat a lady; at that time in my life, and what I had brought on myself, I needed a friend. We stayed there for two hours at the bar drinking and talking. The person who I was waiting on never showed up. The stranger and I became friends, and he was there for me.

I never wanted to see Levi again in my life. His brother called me the night before my court date; and said Levi was out of town. I told him to tell his brother that I never wanted to see him again because number one, he was not out of town; number two, he is a big liar; and number three, he stole from me big time. I was friends with his entire family so I thought.

On my court day, I went to court by myself. No one was there with me. I was sure I was going to walk out of court. By me being on probation, my p.o said that the judge was not happy with the amount of restitution I had paid back so far and she wanted more. I said, "Ok, I'll start paying back more." I really was sure I was walking out of court. My attorney also had me thinking I was going to get another chance, she was also there. She had to read before the judge about my dirty urine. By the time I was in court, my urine was clean. The judge asked me what I had to say; I lied and said,

Your honor, I have not used any drugs. All I know is I was seeing this man who did not have my best interest in hand. By the time I found out what he was doing to me, it was too late. He told my p.o someone else dropped my urine for me and that was a lie. He was looking to make me go back to the penitentiary. I caught him putting something in my drink. There is no telling how long he was doing these things to me. He shot up drugs." The judge said, "So you mean to tell me, Doris, that you have not been using any drugs? I said, "No, Your Honor, not since you put me on probation."

The judge immediately got so angry at me, and she said, "Your men problems are not my fault. That's your fault and a personal problem for you to stand in front of me and say you have not been using drugs. Treatment would not be in your best interest." I responded, I will still be willing to go for treatment because drugs in the past were in my system, and I have been around people that use." "Treatment is for users," she said. I felt like a complete fool. I was standing there wishing I had not lied, like my friend had told me to tell the truth. I went into the court room lying big time, and the judge knew that. I wish I could have taken it all back, and I could have, but pride got in the way. It cost me three years in prison. She said, "Is there anything else you want to tell me?" My mind had completely left me at that monument. I do not remember what she said to me. She said "I sentence you one year for this, one year for that and also a year for this as well." She threw the book at me. All charges were run concurrently. I did not really know how much time I ended up with. I was saying, "You're Honor, Your Honor. She got up, looked at me, and walked away as if she was saying, "You Fool, all you had to do was to tell the truth, and I would have gotten you some help." I stood there and lied in the judge's face, and she had no mercy on me.

The deputies were standing behind me ready to escort me to the back and lock me up. I told them my coat was on the seat. The deputy said, "I will bring it to you." I asked my attorney what I was supposed to do about my household goods, my car, and all my business that I did not have time to take care of. She said I would have to call some of my people to handle it for me. She did not ask the judge to give me time to handle my business; she did not even talk up for me. I guess not after I had lied, and I do not think anyone expected me to lie. That is just how stupid I was thinking I was so smart. The only thing my attorney did ask the judge was to allow me my time that I had spent in the county jail. I was on probation and she granted me that time as well. The judge also said to transport her as soon as possible to the Ohio Reformatory for Woman. My mouth dropped wide open. It still had not hit me yet that I was on my way back to the penitentiary. After ten years I just could not believe it. While I was sitting in that little room in back of the courtroom where they had left me for twenty minutes, I was thinking my whole world had caved in on me right before my eyes. I was dressed very nicely in court, trying to make an impression. I had all my hair pulled back with a black bow on the back of my hair, a two piece skirt suit. The jacket was black and purple, double breasted with gold buttons fastened high up to the neck the skirt was black. It was a very executive suit. I also had on purple shoes. They had a bow in the back and I had on a black leather coat

As I was walking down the long corridor, I asked the c o how much time I actually had; she said, "Three years." I broke down then, but I still could not cry as big as a cry baby I was. The tears would not come out. All I kept on saying is why I had to lie. I sat in the Pod all day with the other ladies until the c o's dressed us in the favored blue outfits. While we were waiting to be booked in again, we could use the phone. I had to call home and tell my family I would be going away for a while, and they had to take care of all my business for me. My mother was at work. This was 10:00 in the morning on July 22, 1992. I talked to my father who sounded very sad and upset, for one because I did not let the family know I was in trouble. I told my father that Mom had to go over to my apartment at once and make arrangements to get my things out of the house because I felt Levi was going to break into my house the same day and clean me out. I did not put anything passed him. I told Dad that Mom had seen him before, and she did not like him. Mom always knows best. She really did not like me with him because he was such a "dog". He had called down to court to find out what had happened to me. He sent some fat lady to my house, and lucky my mom was there. The lady told my mother she heard that I wanted to rent my apartment out. My mother said that it did not sound like anything my daughter would say. It sounded like a lie. He put some of his no good friends up to doing that. I felt so badly by putting my mother up to cleaning my house out; however, I did not think I was going away. I was a very private person who stayed in trouble.

My mother was on top of my business. No one could run any nonsense under her and get away with it. Years later, things and people showed me that so many people in the world are not right. On the other hand there are so many of those who are. Those are the people I choose to be around today. My nephew Grant told me Levi called him and told him how much time I had. Levi was always up to no good. He acted like he cared so much about me. He cared about what he could get, and he thought everyone else was so stupid. He told my nephew to tell me to call him, but I never did because I thought it was a trap that he was trying to put me into a "Trick bag".

I sat in the county jail a week before I rode to Marysville penitentiary in Marysville, Ohio. One morning I was woken up at 4:00 a.m., and I was told to pack it up. I tried to throw all negative things out of my mind to get ready to pull all the time I had in front of me. During that week I was still making calls in Cleveland. I called my ex-men Jo, Ira, and Neil to let them know that I would be gone for a while and what my sentence was. Neil was in Georgia. He told me he would look out for me by sending me money from time-to-time to my mother. Ira was very old and sickly; he did tell me to call him anytime to let him know what was going on with me. The second time I called him, he stopped accepting my calls. He stated that the telephone calls were $ 3.00 and that was too much for him to accept. I told him I will pray for us both for God to give us wisdom, strength, and courage. I told him to be good, and I would not be troubling him anymore. When a person goes to jail, sometimes it seems like the whole world is against him or her. I was talking to my mother every day until I rode to Marysville. It took my family a few days to clean my house out; they did not pack my things like I would have, but she had done the best she could. I did my time and went back home. I got home, and my things were all messed up.

I had this piece of furniture I had gotten from Germany which was called a "Shrunk". It was like a big wall unit but better. It covered the entire wall and came in three pieces; in the middle there was a china cabinet with a drawer at the bottom; the two end pieces were just drawers, a book shelf, a place to put pictures, and a bar was on one end.

The saying about Germany was you would leave with one of three things-a baby, a shrunk, or a cuckoo clock. I said it will not be a shrunk because they are too big; it will not be a cuckoo clock because I never liked them coo-cooing all the time, and I was hoping it would have been a baby. I so badly wanted a baby by my husband. It was a shrunk I left Germany with; I did not see anything my family done until I returned home after three years. The shrunk grew on me and it had never been taken apart.

At first, my mother had said that my sisters were going to divide the shrunk and everybody takes a piece. My sisters had a home full of furniture of their own. My family did not have room to put my belongings. My mother's house was full as well. They disassembled my shrunk piece by piece. There had to be a lot of pieces. I thought, "How could they possibly keep up with those many pieces. Did they care about keeping up with my stuff?" I did not think they really cared.

Mom gave my carpet away that I had in my two bedrooms to one of my brother's friends who was helping them move. She had to pay the helpers. She claimed no one had any money to pay the help. I understood. If it had of been my baby sister's stuff; mom would have saved it all. It was hard to get family members to help me. There were at least six family members who could have helped but they did not want to. I remember my brother-in-law asked me if I felt badly that I put that onto my mother to come in my house and have to move my things out because I had gone to jail. I felt he had stepped over his boundaries. Sure I felt badly, and that was not his place to say. He had a lot of nerves asking me that. My mother got smart with me and said if I did not like the way she was doing things, I could come home and do it myself. I cried about that and told her how badly she had hurt me by saying that. Then she said the family will just have to help me get more stuff when I get out. She was just saying that. I knew when the time came for me to get the new carpet; mom would talk a new and different tune. She probably would say something about how much money I owe her. My mother knew damn well I could not come home and do anything. That is where I get my smart mouth from.

My mother made me feel like a stepchild a lot. When I did talk to Mom on the telephone from time-to-time, I asked her to put some money on my books. I just never understood why it was so hard for her to do things for me. She used to tell me things like, "We did not put you in jail." She was the only one saying that. I know no one put me into jail but myself. She acted like she had never made a mistake in her life. That is not true; *everyone* makes mistakes--some big, others small; some people get caught.

As time went by, my mom's negativity to me got a little easier; she had a heart and started doing things for me while I was locked up. I had tried over and over to change my lifestyle because I never wanted to go back to prison. At times I did not know what was wrong with me.

That first week of me being locked up was hard; after Mom and the family got my things out of my house, the time got a little easier. I had to thank God because things could have really been worse. I feel my family could have saved my car. It was a five speed; I was six months shy from paying it off. I had $500 dollar wheels on my car with wheels locks. My family said no one could drive a stick shift car. That was a lie; my brother-in-law could for one, and my brother could also drive a stick shift car. I was not that loved by my family. They let my car get repossessed. Then I found out that my sister and brother-in law were about to lose their house. Mom stepped up and paid for that, and I was not supposed to find that out. They knew that would have broken my heart just like it did. Somebody "let the cat out the bag". My car was almost new. My nephew was going to keep the car for me, pay it off, and learn how to drive it. I think my mother and my sister talked him out of doing that.

As I am sitting at my computer typing this material, bad things are popping up in my life that I made it through. I am getting very angry at some of the things that I am reliving, and some of the things I am remembering as I am typing on how badly I was treated coming up as a young woman. Life has really showed me how much I have grown today. Like I was told some thirty years ago, *I am a winner, and a* very strong woman.

Everybody was saying that they would help me get a car when I got out. I knew that was a lie. I had struggled with that car note for three years. I managed with the Lord's help to keep my car; it almost got repossessed three times. The Lord made a way for me to hold onto it. I had never in my life had anything repossessed. That just goes to show how easy something can be lost that took so long to accomplish. I had gotten in my mind the only way I was going to do the time was not talk to my family so much.

I had started talking to some of the girls in the county jail with me about Marysville and how I hated going back through WCAC which was admissions. This girl told me that they did not have that anymore. I was glad to hear that. I had not been back to Mary's House as it was called in ten years. I felt good staying out of the penitentiary for ten years. I got too over confident that I had it made, but in reality I was still a sick person who had to be very careful. I said, "Here I go again."

I was told that admissions were only two weeks, and it was on the farm; and it was called Marysville or Mary's House. Some ladies got to the penitentiary and they did not stay out a long time before they went right back in. During my stay of three years, I saw many women come back through that "Revolving door." I had said that was not going to be me. Three years "knocked sparks out my ass" so I thought. Everything happens for a reason. I was filling out papers to get my felonies forgiven.

I was in community college off and on forever seen like. I did not know what I wanted to do or how I was going to get it done. My deceased sister used to tell me all the time what God had done for her and that He would do the same thing for me. As usual, I did not see that nor did I believe it. My life was really on the way to total destruction. God had to make His child "Me" see what I was doing to myself. I got caught up in things that never should have taken place.

Once I got to Marysville, admission was a brand new building that had been built. It looked more like the men's jail cells or something you see on television. There were two women to a room. It was a big improvement to me from what I was used to. The rules were pretty much the same from back in the day. We had to walk what was called the line to meals and everywhere else we went. Walking the line meant a straight line or follow the yellow bricks, or it was just the path we had to walk. If by chance we got off the line, there were consequences such as a ticket, and if we got too many tickets, it could have meant "The hole" which was just a cell by yourself and meals were delivered to you.

I started asking around for Black cat and if she was still there. I was told she got out and came back. I was very surprised she was there on the farm. I got a message to her that Doris was back. I knew she would come to breakfast to see me. One morning going to breakfast, there was this Black lady standing with this white woman on the wall in the back of the lunch room; for some reason I focused right on them. Then I looked away. She called me by name very loudly because she knew I did not realize it was her. I looked at her again really hardly and moved my lips and said, "Black Cat". She shook her head "Yes." I could not talk to her because I was not out in population yet, and we could not mingle with the other ladies. I went on and sat down with my tray of breakfast, nodding my head back at her. I was smiling because I was happy to see her, to know she was not dead.

I did not get a telephone call until after the first week, and I called home to ask about someone sending me some money. My mother was not home; my father started preaching at me, talking a lot of negative stuff. I was so surprised because they had not heard from me in a while, and I thought they would be glad to hear from me to know how I was getting along. They had no idea what a person goes through in prison. All my parents knew was that they had never been locked up. As usual we started arguing, and my father hung up the phone. My father said I should have called when my mother was home. I did not know when my mother was home and when she was not; she stayed gone a lot. I asked about my dog, Terri. I missed her. I also asked about all my stuff in my house. Dad hung up the telephone on me it deeply hurt me to my heart. I went back to my room and cried. I did not get to use the phone until another week. Daddy had failed to realize that I had no control of when I was allowed to make a phone call. I had to be the understanding one and humble myself; I did not want him hanging up on me anymore.

After being in admissions for two weeks, we went into population. This time I was in B quarters. I got lucky and got a two-person room. I had no complaints. My roommate was "cool", and she had a television. I had the top bunk which was ok. I was young. She and I got along greatly. My roommate told me that every roommate she had had did not stay any more than two weeks. I said, "Why is that?" She said either they get shipped to the honor camp, pre-released in Cleveland, or pre-released in Columbus. I did not want to go home to pre-release in Cleveland because that was too close to home. I wanted to stay right there in Marysville to do my time, knowing I had no choice in the matter to me they had more to offer a person doing a lot of time. I did not know about all the different programs they had to offer.

When I was in Marysville doing eight months the first time, I was in OPI working as a power sewing machine operator doing piece work. OPI is Ohio Penal Industries. I would never forget the employee who was in charge because her name was the same as the elementary school I attended. I wrote a kite which was a note, asking to come back. The ladies in OPI income was up to a hundred dollars a month state pay which was the highest paying jog on the farm doing piece work. I ended up dropping her kite after kite; she never got back with me to "Say "Yes," or "No." If I had stayed there long enough, I was going to keep on dropping kites until I got back into OPI. I was told that there were no openings. The prison was so overcrowded until there were no jobs for the new ladies to do. Therefore, I was called a "Housekeeper," and I had to stay around the cottage working hours to do whatever they told me to do which could consist of anything from mopping the floor to running errands, and going in the yard picking up cigarettes butts. In B-cottage we had our own yard; therefore, we did not have to share a yard with other inmates. We had to be up by 8a.m., dressed, and ready to go to work. If we wanted to eat breakfast, we had to be up before that. Usually I worked for an hour, and then I went back to my room to lie down and watch television until they were looking for me. Three weeks later, I rode to Cleveland via pre-release. I could not understand why they rode me to my home to do three years. I was very upset about that. The ride was very long; I had to wear shackles on my feet. I had seen this place all the time off the freeway and on the street; I had no idea that it was a prison. I had heard it used to be the men's pre-release. A friend of mine said he did his last six months there. The pre-release change over to the women's pre-release. This was my second time being locked up my first and last time at pre-release.

I was looking really badly upon arriving at what was called NEPRC for North East Pre-Release Center. I did not stay at Maryville long enough to go to the beauty shop. All the products that were needed to do hair were sold at the commissary. There were enough ladies who did hair for a small fee. We could get any kind of style we wanted. I was still wearing a Jerry Curl. I would change up my hair duos sometimes and get finger waves, and then I would go to work at CFS which was the kitchen, to sweat my finger waves out. I had to make the best of it because that is what I got assigned to which they signed everybody to the kitchen when first getting to pre-release. The hours were long and the state pay was low. My hours were 11:30a.m. To 6:30p.m. A lot of the time, if the kitchen was cleaned up really well and everything shining, we got to leave a half hour early. I worked in pots and pans; I did my job, and the lazy women had to work as well. I had said to the inmates who I was working with that "I will not do all of the work, none of us want to do this work." If I had to work, everybody else is going to do the same thing. I stayed in pots and pans for thirty days, until there was an opening came available; I was told a line job was mine as a line servicer. Sometimes, I am a serious person about life. People did not know how to take me. I think I am a well-liked person. I do not like noisy people getting into my business; most of the time that is not the case. People want to know what is going on so they can talk.

Lieutenant Williams was the boss over the ladies at CFS. He was hard on all the hard-working ladies such as me. One day he brought me in some sweet rolls and told me to hide them and I did; they were nice and hot. I took them back to my room, heated and ate them. I ate them by myself. By me starting on the line a day before, I was made to still clean the pots and pans that day; I was really upset about that. I told lieutenant Williams that was not fair for me to have to clean the line and pots and pans. All the ladies were new in pots and pans; they did not know what they were doing. The pots and pans were stacked up very high. I said, "Oh my God! What have you all been doing back here? "I see nothing has been done." When I was in pots and pans, it was never that much stuff backed up like that." I used to run pots and pans and Lt. knew I was fast. He wanted me to go ahead and help them clean the pots and pans and train the new ladies. I trained them and told them that the pots and pans had to be organized first, or they would always be behind and backed up. One lady scraped the pots and pans, one washed, one dried, one put them up, and one went up front on the line to get the dirty pots and pans; then we rotated and took turns so one lady did not have to do the same thing all the time. The ladies could not thank me enough, although I had done double work that day.

On the line my boss was Ms. Lawson, Ms. Harrison, and a new C.O. named Ms. Wilson. Ms. Lawson was very sweet; she did many favors for us inmates; some ladies made it hard because a rumor was that an inmate was messing around with one of the guards. They put the inmate in the hole and then shipped her back to Marysville. Ms. Harrison was ok, she hated to give us a break; she used to just make us stay around CFS when we had nothing to do; we stayed there too many hours out of a day. Ms. Harrison trained Ms. Wilson; therefore, she did not like giving us a break either. After Ms. Wilson learned her job, she started giving us breaks, and we were happy about that. We also got away with much stuff with Ms. Wilson. She thought she was watching us, but the hand is faster than the eye. We walked out of CFS with all kinds of food under Ms. Wilson's shift. Ms. Wilson caught me with three cookies one time; I had already gotten two dozen and put them up. It was like that on ice cream, cake, sugar, and anything else we wanted to sell to the ladies once we got back to our cottages. The ladies used some of the seasonings to cook with that we got from CFS at the cottages when they did not want to go to CFS.

I got along with just about everybody. Working on the line servicing the ladies' meals was very enjoyable at times. When Joan and myself were working side-by-side on the line, Joan used to tell the inmates coming through the line, if they do not want the food, do not eat it; "You bitches think you all are at the Red Lobster somewhere. This is not having it your way." I used to laugh. Joan did not care what she said to people; she and I were roommates. During that time she and I got very close. She and I were on the line, and I used to push the ladies to work faster by telling them, "Come on ladies, let's pick the pace up, or let's move it ladies, we are backed up;" I would say that really loudly. The line used to be fifty or better strong outside of the kitchen I used to tell whichever c.o. was there with us not to put a particular lady on the line because she worked too slowly and would only slow us down. I suggested that whoever was slow to be the runner or give her something else to do. Everybody knew I used to push to get the six hundred plus total women fed and back to their cottages so we could clean up and go back to our own cottages. We also used to play and clown on the line at times to make our day go on by.

My ninety days were up, and I could get released from CFS into another job. I was reclassified to a porter job. I was on first shift which was 8am to 2pm. I loved that job; however, I was living in cottage H and working in L. I had to keep reporting back and forth to work after count had cleared for lunch. I sat around and did nothing most of the time. I did not want to work that hard for twenty dollars a month state pay. In the beginning we had to work very hard when I was in CFS. Things got better as time passed.

My break came, my boss Mrs. Forest asked me if I wanted to move over to L unit since I was working there, she wanted all her porters together. I told her yes I will move. God knows best all the time. L unit would be much nicer and quitter in that cottage. I wrote all the time, every time I got a chance, I always had paper and a pencil in my hand. I needed the quiet time to think, and by me living where I work, I did not have to keep running back and forth to work. I wanted to get into a two-person room. I have always had a four person room, too many women; I had to deal with it because I had no other choice.

When I first got to North East Pre-Release they had me in L unit for three days; at that time L unit was admissions. I was in L 222. Then I moved to H unit room 236; two months later, I moved back to L222 the same room, the same bed. I said what is it about room 222; I enjoyed my room in L because I was right up front where I could see everything, I had a good view of the freeway, the Akron sign that said Akron 77 south, I could see all the visitors as they came and left. My window was right by the dance yard that was for us inmates to dance in the summer. Most of all I was right by the window where I got a good breeze at night. My new roommates and I got along pretty good. When there are four ladies to a room there is always going to be some kind of mess. One of my new roommates also had a cut on her face; I asked her what had happen. She said, she was a hoe, and wanted some dope but she wanted to get one more trick for the night; so she could have enough money to get more dope. This was a Black man who all the hoes knew; he told her to "Get in the car and give him some head," she did, as she was giving him head he took out a razor and cut her face for no reason at least that is what she said. She said "Dam man you did not have to do that." she asked him if he had a towel or something to put on her face to help stop the bleeding. It was bleeding pretty badly she said. He told her to "Get out of his car with her bleeding ass all on my shit I will have to get cleaned." Come to find out she had said that her trick had killed a friend of hers two nights ago. She was debating rather to go to the hospital right them or stop first by the dope house, bleeding like a pig, half her face was gone and she were talking about getting hi. She was about two blocks from the hospital and two blocks from the dope house. She did the right thing and went on to the hospital. She had to go back to her county to testify against her trick that cut her face. He was facing murder for her friend and he had charges pending for her as well.

Some of the ladies who looked old were not that old. There was this one lady who everybody called her "Granny"; she was one of my roommates who were only fourth-eight years old. I said, no way I would allow anyone to call me Granny at that age. She was not even ten years older than me. Granny had had a very hard life. All she talked about was drinking alcohol. She said one time she drank so much until her wig sat on her head sideways, and that she did not give a dam. She really was a very sweet person, but she got on my nerves a lot because I could be writing or listening to my music, and she would want to talk and ask me the same questions repeatedly. She could never remember anything. I had to take her over to M building to ask them to please give her a pair of tennis shoes because she was walking on the ground. They gave the shoes to her after they saw the ones she was wearing. She was so happy. I had to give her wash rags because she would lose them and not know where her wash rag was. I told her it does not do any good to give her anything because she never knows what had happened to it. Her socks were so nasty and black; I told her to throw them away; I gave her some of my socks. I told her I did not see why she wore wigs. She had pretty hair. The ladies were getting ready to put a jerry curl in Granny hair knowing she would not keep it up. As long as I was her roommate, I would help her. Another inmate was also in the room with us, she went to the hole for stealing state clothes. The order came from the captain to lock her up. She had to take her rollers out her hair, and she had to pack up all of her stuff because she would not come back to our room after getting out of the hole.

The c o's had searched her state clothes; we were only supposed to have one drawer; Ms. Hicks had two, and she like a dummy showed the c o's her two drawers. She had at least ten pair of state pants, ten skirts, and six pair of shorts and twenty pair of underwear, which she was not supposed to have. All her state underwear was white. Apparently the shorts had been reported missing, and she worked in clothing exchange. She had never been to the hole; therefore, she did not know what to expect--only what the c.o had told her. The hole is a jail cell with a bunk bed. The light stays on all day and night, and the inmate cannot come out until she serviced her time. Sometimes the c.o would let the inmate walk around the yard to get a little exercise depending on how many days she had in the hole. She was allowed her cigarettes if she had any, although a lighter was not allowed; however, she could have matches. The only thing she could take to the hole with her was paper to write, ink pens, envelopes, mailing stamps, hair grease, comb, brush, one pair of underwear, all her bed linen, one pair of stocks and three pieces of reading materials. She had to stay in the hold at least seven days; then she would go in front of the RIB board at that time it would determine if she got more time in the hole or let her out.

I did not like ladies who shopped only on state pay once a month because they used to ask for everything, and sometimes the answer had to be no because I would run out trying to take care of another person. If I did give things, I had to charge them two for one for whatever they wanted.

I was determined to get me a two person room. Then I really would be ok because I had my own television, radio and Walkman. I never needed to go out of my room unless I wanted to. The ladies always kept up a lot of negative activities, as I call it shit starters. I was not on all that mess and I did not want to be involved with it. I was glad that I wrote all the time. Every time someone saw me I was writing. One lady had said to me. "Every time I see you, you are always writing you must want to be a writer." I said something like that. This other lady asked me if I ever stepped out of my room; I said, "Yes," when I wanted to eat or just want to go outside and "Kick it" for a while to get some fresh air.

This one inmate was a snitch. She always used to sit around and listen to people talk, then go back and, repeat what she had heard and get the facts wrong every time. She stayed in the c.os face all the time. She had an odor about herself and she did not like taking showers. I went to the c.o on her to make her wash her butt.

Another of my roommates who worked in commissary thought she was privileged but she was still an inmate at the end of the day. She shopped a day before we did. She was thirty six years old, a little younger than me. She too lived a hard life; someone rearranged one side of her face; there was a long cut on one side. She thought she was super fine as wine, but in reality, she was ugly. In the winter of 1992, we had a lot of trouble out of her. It got pretty hot in our room at times; we used to plug the vent up to stop some of the heat from coming in. She was the only one in the room talking about it is a fire hazard, so she used to unplug the vent. I plugged it back up. She and I went through that most of the winter. Then it was a problem with the lights being on, on the weekend. We could stay up all night and watch movies if we wanted to out in the television room. She wanted the lights to stay on in our room all night, and we told her that there were four women in this room, and the majority rules. One night one of the other roommates got tired of her and told her that if she touches the light one more time, she was going to beat her up and fix the other side of her face so both sides will match. She got a little scared. I was on my bed laughing. Someone else other than I stood up to her.

Another night I could not take any more of the intense heat. I was on the top bunk, and I could not breathe since heat rises. I was stopped up; I had slept on the floor for three nights straight. I said, "Forget this mess." I plugged the vent up; it was about 1:00 a.m., and I could not sleep, and I refused to get on the floor again. The trouble maker roommate unplugged the vent. She and I kept going back and forth with plugging and unplugging it. She unplugged the vent one time too many. I jumped off my bunk and pulled the chair away from under her, and she hit the floor. The chair went one way and she went another. She got up off the floor and said, "Doris, as long as you live, do not ever pull a chair from under me again." I said, "What are you going to do about it?" She said, "I need to kick your ass." I told her to bring it on; I said, "If you touch it again, I will do the same thing and pull the chair." She went running out into the hallway as if someone was killing her calling for the c.o. The c.o came into the room asking what was going on.

I let her do all the talking. When she got finished, I said, "Sir, I do not know why she is lying." I said she fell out of the chair. The roommates had my back because we were tired of her mess. The c.o did not see it, so it was her word against ours. I never had disliked a person as much as her. She did not get along with anyone. Other roommates used to mess with her for the fun of it. One of the roommates told her she was going to wake up one morning with no hair. We all probably would have gotten into trouble for that if we did not tell who had done it; so I talked her out of doing that one. She went and told the c.o because she was scared. A black woman would have gotten hung up to dry for messing with a white woman in prison; they had a lot of mouth, well so did a lot of blacks. Some c.o's were fair about different situations with a Black and white woman. Then other c.o would let a Black get away with murder; they all had their favored I had to ask for a room change because I would have ended up hurting her real badly and I wanted to finish my time and go home. Misery loves company and I had to stop feeding into other inmates mess.

One night my new roommates and I had stayed up all night having fun singing, dancing, and eating, of course it was on the weekend where the next morning we did not have to get up early if we did not want to. One of my roommates was the only one who had to go to work Saturday morning. She got up very early and turned the lights on to wake the rest of us up. That was dirty of her. We all were trying to pay the lights no attentions because she was trying to pay us back for the night before. No one told her to try and hang with us when she knew she had to go to work the next morning. The next night we did the exactly the same thing. The girl next door wanted to join us she called herself a bull dagger who love women. Smith started liking my roommate, Smith use to play with her all the time. Joan use to laugh and say girl I have told you that I am strictly dickey. Every time Joan would say that I laugh, it was so funny to me; that did not stop Smith she kept on playing with Joan because she knew she liked it. Joan said she really did not like that what she was doing to her; I told her if she did not like what she was doing she should have stopped it and not play with Smith because she was sending her mixed signs. Joan is dead today as well as Smith.

One night Smith got Joan behind the door and was humping on her, Joan was fighting her off laughing all at the same time; Joan was saying stop, stop girl I have told you I am strictly dickey; Smith said so what does that mean to me. Another night Joan, sat straight up on her bunk, she was in a deep sleep, it was Smith, pulling her grown up, and we saw her panties; thank God she had underwear on. Joan laugh we all laugh as well. Then Joan told Smith again I have told you to stop doing shit like that. Smith continued to pay Joan no attention at all. Women were talking to women all over the camp; I guess that was the going thing. It was not for me. All I did was sell my contraband card to the ladies for commissary.

Shortly after I got to North East Pre-Release Center the ladies were ordering Mr. Hero that was around August 1992. I had no money on my books so I had to look at everybody eat; no one offer the new ladies a smell nor let anyone smell a small piece of their Mr. Hero's. The second time we ordered Mr. Hero's I made sure I had money on the books. Mr. Hero's was a treat for us ladies.

After being at NEPRC for a month, I saw one of my very close friends I use to hang with on the street because her boyfriend and my boyfriend were best of friends in high school; she and I lived across town from each other. She lived in East Cleveland and I lived in Garfield, Heights. The four of us always hung out together. She said she was really shocked to see me locked up. She and I use to hand dance back in the day with our men; us four use to practice what we were going to do to show off in wreck. We were good hand dancers. I was there when her first baby was born. When I first saw her I had to grab and hug her. She thought I never got into any trouble. She really did not know me because I stayed in trouble. She looked out for me because I did not know anyone in prison. She said she did not know anyone either when she first got locked up. She was very out spoken and made friends easy I did not. Many people go to prison knowing each other from the street because they were in a circle together.

On Memorial Day 1992 we ate steak, every year the prison also gave the inmates like a little carnival for the ladies, we ate so good that day until some of the ladies got sick. We had a lot of fun, we had games like the wheel of fortune, black jack, and a few others games, we could play for candy bars, and matrix make up which I loved. They also gave us a big bag of popcorn. We had a dancing contest; I did not get in that because the girls were dancing as if they were in the club on the pole. That was like hoe dancing to me. Then to top everything off, we had October fest where each cottage made something for display, and present in front of the entire camp; my cottage won. Our prize was every woman in the cottage got a fried chicken dinner. It was delivered to us that evening. Everyone was so full until we could not enjoy it because of all the food we had eaten earlier that day. Inmates were getting sick from stuffing the food down.

My first Christmas came around I was so home sick and lonely. It was a wonderful day, the sun was shining bright, and the ground was barely covered with snow; I called home to wish everyone a Merry Christmas, I talked to my little nephew, who was three years old at the time. He said thank you auntie Jean for my gift. The staff at the prison sent all the kids a gift so I put his name in the basket to get a Christmas gift. My nephew and niece received a gift from me. We had a wonderful lunch, the menu was turkey, dressing, cranberry sauce, dinner rolls, potato salad which was nothing like as good as I make, green beans and a juice; it was very filling, everyone had dressed up for the occasion. On Christmas Eve everyone received a care package containing tooth paste, tooth brushy, soap, an apple, an orange, four candy canes, and a bottle of matrix hair spray which was for white people. After we ate lunch our day was over, everything went back to normal pretty much. Everyone sat around the rest of the day playing cards or watching television. Our dinner that day was pretty sorry. Any time we had a good lunch, dinner would be a sandwiches or something. The next day was my birthday, which was December 26. I got a card from my mother, and my sister Ola which I got from her every year with $50.00 on my books; that always lifted my spirits up. Later, that evening some of the girls did say happy birthday to me. A lot of the girls use to cook for their birthday. I did not; I did not have the food to do that. I was just glad to see another year in which I had behind me.

It was New Year's Eve, at 12 midnight I rain up and down the halls saying Happy New Years, the co did not say anything, she let us have our fun. My roommates and I stayed up half the night dancing, cracking jokes, and having fun. The noise from our room continued until someone went to the c o complaining about the noise in my room the co asked us to keep the noise down because others were trying to sleep. New Year's Day was not too much because everyone on staff was at home with their families. There was a skeleton crew on staff; our meals that day were pretty sorry. It was another lonely day. Winter of 1992 was my first year being locked up at NEPRC. Winter started late, it did not come in good until the beginning of 1993, even then it was a light snow on the ground, we had a few bad days with thunder storms, but the snow crew stayed out almost 24 hours they did have the girls in shifts. Some of the girls got out and mad snowmen in the front yard.

I was so glad to see spring roll around; the trees and the grass started to turn green, a sign that spring was on its way. I would be leaving prison this year so I thought. The sun was shining so bright, the rays of the sun gave me so much energy. A lot of the white inmates were lying in the sun, trying to get them a tan, the air even smelled clean and light.

Since the recreation lady left last year there were not any more actives. We used to play bingo twice a month, take pictures every week, also had dancing. Last year we were supposed to get roller skates to skate around the walk jog that was the perfect skating ring; that never happened, we also was supposed to have jazz-a-size, that never happen either.

April 11, Easter Sunday, us ladies, had a real nice lunch once again as we usually had on the holiday. About 7:00 pm that evening, everyone got locked down; we did not know what was going on or why we were being lock down. Something had happen. A half-hour later, the warden came around to each unit and said the reason we had to be locked down was because there had been a hostage situation in Lucasville, which is a maxims prison security for men in Southern Ohio. All the prisons were locked down, therefore, we did not go to work on Monday, no school, no activates, nothing was moving on the camp. Wherever we had to go on the grounds, we had to be escorted. We had to be escorted to meals. The only thing those who had doctor's appointments had been kept; and they were escorted there by the co. I really did not care about the lock down because I had my own television, Walkman, and a watch. I was straight; I could have stayed in my room, and got me some rest. This was a nationwide alert of all penitentiaries all over the world. "The news had said guards had been hurt." Monday April 13, 1993 was a regular working day for us, we could go outside and do the things we were doing before the lock down; but every day on the news they were talking about the hostages and what was going on in Lucasville. The last thing I heard was six hostages, who were guards, had been killed, and the inmates were killing up their own people. One of the ladies at NEPRC brother was one of the inmates who got killed at Lucasville that was a very sad occasion. Everyone was giving her their condolences; she did go to her brother funeral, they were from Akron, Ohio. There was a ride that came in from Marysville shortly after the hostage's situation. The ladies came from maximum security, they said they were "Locked down an entire week and they too had to get escort to meals and they could not go anywhere else. I ended up calling my family shortly after all that had happen because I knew my family had heard about the situation on the news. I just wanted to tell them I was alright.

My state of mind mentally, physically, and socially were ok until I called home, and my mother start talking that negative talk to me, about I put myself in prison, she really thought she were helping me, but in reality she was hurting me bad deep down inside of me. My mother was crushing my spirits. I really think she did not know any better, so I had to try and forgive her, for she did not know any better. All I wanted from my parents was a little moral support. Do not get me wrong I am very grateful, because I could have been dead. By the grace of God and his mercy my time has not been that bad this far. I am grateful, and not complaining because everything I asked my family to do such as, I need clothes, or money or whatever; they did try to help me out the best they could. I understand, it is not my family fault, I am in prison. My family has their lives to live, and life goes on. Time does not stop for any one. I once told my mother she did not understand all the mentally, and emotional abuse we have to take being locked up. I had to get up in the mornings, when they said get up, I had to go to bed when they said go to bed, I had to take orders, If I like it or not. If orders was not obeyed, that maybe would of been hold time, fighting was hold time, and etc. I had to keep my force on my dreams, wants, and desires. A lot of things my mother said to me hurt me to my heart, and she was in her right state of mind. Mom was just very uneducated. I could have not gotten through my time if it was not for the will of "GOD." He is the one who kept me strong threw it all, no matter what came my way;

I fell down and got back up over and over again until now I am ready to go forward with my life and not ever look back unless I am helping someone else.

On Sunday, May 2ᵗʰ 1993 the co's had their family day and they brought their families to the prison; to see the way the inmates live. One of my favorite co who was in food service got the same last name as I. He had his wife and son with him. He was a very intelligent bright little boy, and he was very handsome. He kept a hold to his daddy leg. I went up to him and knelled down beside him, and said hi, he waved at me, I said oh you cannot talk, he shook his head yes, and said yes, I can talk. I said, and then what is your name? He said Isaac, I said, that is a nice name, and how old are you? He said "Four yours old. "I then said your mother have you dressed very nice, and you also smell good. He said thank you. He grabbed his daddy leg again, as to say I am tired of talking to you now. Lieutenant Williams was dressed very nice in all his red, he really was too dark to have on all red. His wife had on a ring that would blind you, if you stared at it long enough. It was sparking so bright; I had to grab her hand, and ask her may I look at it real close, she said sure, and told me it was her anniversary gift from her husband, a very beautiful gift indeed it was. I said to Mr. Williams, that's right you take good care of your wife, he smiled, it might have been about 3 carts or so; I was scared to ask. Diamonds were all over the ring with one big diamond in the center. Family day for the co's was very enjoyable, meeting and talking to the staff family.

On May 18ᵗʰ 1993 my best friend Beverly leaves this morning. I had said when she left I really was going to be lonely because she was the only reason I went outside as much as I did, she use to come get me a lot of times to walk. She and I were together much as possible. We kept each other motivated. I had to talk about Beverly because she was very stingy and she did not like sharing with me. She could have got anything from me that I had. I use to help her out a lot when we shopped, and if she was short, and I had the money, she had it. I had trouble with her not wanting to pay me back. She just always thought she was slick. I got her out of her stingy un-selfish ways. That morning I helped Beverly take her things over to M-building to get checked out.

She looked very nice leaving NEPRC. She had on a pair of nice black pants, black top, tennis shoes, and her hair had just been done that morning. She wore her hair one side long, the other side was short. That style fitted her face. As she and I went to the M-building looking at each other lost for words, we managed to talk a minute. I told her to be good, stay out of trouble, and most of all not to come back. I gave her a big hug, water was in my eyes. She said Jean do not cry you will be out soon. I hated to see her leave me there, but that is how it was. She said she would write by the end of the week; she even said she should have her car by then. She said she would go see my Lawyer to see if I could get out before July of 1995. I gave her all my paper work I had concerning my case to give to the lawyer to see if she could get me out. I had no reason not to believe her; however, I thought I knew her, but I really knew nothing about her. I truly thought she was going to take care of my business like she said. What I failed to realize that people talk shit when they are locked up. I did not like that, and that is why I guess I did not trusted people. People in prison do not mean what they say, it just sounds good; once they are on the street, free again they forget all about what they had said until they get into trouble again.

Beverly wanted me to stay with her until she left, I could not, I had to report to work. I went to work and ask Mr. Pete who was the co on duty that morning and if I could go back and see Beverly off? He said yes. He told me just to come back, I said ok. That morning it was raining pretty badly I hung around outside by the gate for a while to at least wave good-bye to her once last time. The rain would not allow me to stay outside. I was soak-in-wet. She never came out, so either I had missed her or she was already gone or she still was inside waiting to get released. I went up to my room to change clothes, and to watch from the window; I look out the window just in time, the guard was taking the ladies that were being released from the M-building to the A-building to get their money. It was a total of fifteen women released that morning. Beverly family was waiting at the gate for her. She did not see me because I was in my hallway window where my room was; she never looked up. She hugged her family; they walked on to the car, put her things in the car, and they drove away. That was the last I saw or heard from her until she came back. It had been two weeks since Beverly had left; everybody was asking me if I had heard anything from her. I said no, she probable needed time to get her together, I said. My ex-husband had met her on the street and he told me she did get a car and she let the dope man rent her car for drugs; she should know they never bring your car back when they say. He said she probably would be back there with me. I still had at least two more years.

June 6, 1993 I got a letter from a new pen pal. His sister Janet wanted me to write him, at the time when she asked me; I told her no, because I did not want a pen pal. I found out that most of the pen pal's just needed someone to correspond with while they were locked up. I was not looking for that kind of a relationship. Janet, kept on bugging me trying to convenience me to write her brother, I asked her why me? Out of all these women that are here, why is it you want me to write to your brother? She said in her eyes of what she sees, I was the only one who was real. I have heard that from many people that I am still *genuine* even till today. She also told me that I was down to earth and I was sincere about getting my life together. Janet went on to tell me a little about her brother Ron, she said he is a very nice person. He knows how to treat a lady, and he is a *genuine* person like you Doris. He was about my age, I finally told her ok, I will write him because I got tired of her asking me. When I finally got the letter from him, he seemed to be a pretty cool guy. I still had to remember the fact that we all still were behind bars, and to take no one serious. I also was writing another guy who was in London prison. He got out on June 20, 1993. He was very serious about writing me letters; he said a friend in need is a friend in deed. He had already sent me money on by books. I do not know how he did that but he did. One thing is for sure, he could not ask me for any loving. While we were writing he said, he was not going to forget about me once he got out. Well, that was a lie they all do. I was so insecurity. Today, it is hard for me to trust people because of all the hurt in the past. My pen-pal, from Akron Ohio, gave me a lot of strength and encouragement of my accomplishments he and I had gotten very close by writing and telling each other what is inside of our hearts. We also sent each other pictures of ourselves.

July 14, was yard day; I had never seen nothing like that before in my life, I will never forget that day. I had forgotten that I was in the penitentiary. I thought I was at some kind of an amusement park. There were all kinds of games such as wheel of fortune, bean bag games, dunk the C.O., throw and make a bean bag in the clown mouth, bowling game, basketball game, fish for a prize in a barrel, making the birdy in the basket, pie eating contest, three card molly, and a lot more games. Everyone really enjoyed themselves even the co's. The food was one of the best times we had. The inmates even were allowed to eat all we wanted from 10:30 am to 3:00 pm. How much food could a person consume from that time period? There were inmates being greedy, and afterwards people were throwing up all over the place. We also had water melon, bake beans, cold slaw, hamburgers, hotdogs, cake, pie, Kool-Aid, pop-corn, cotton candy, and snow cones. We could win up to five prizes. The only thing that was missing from the entire event was a few rides, and a few men. The inmates played the co's in a game of basketball, the co's won of course; there were dancing, and the drill team marched; which they had on white t-shirts, red tams on their heads, with beige shorts. Everyone was dressed up for the festivities. No one had to work that day except the cafeteria crew.

CHAPTER TWELVE

Part Two: Half Way Finish
With Three Years

A new year had come January, 25, 1994. I have long forgotten about my dear friend Beverly. I have one more year before I get out. I knew I would see her again in life. My ex-husband had run into Beverly some time ago getting high; she had stated she had just gotten out of North East Pre-Release. He told her his ex-wife was there. She asked him what is her name, he told her, she said, "Yes, I know Jean; she is my best girlfriend, and I was real tight with her while I was there," She happened to had been over to Mike's my ex-husband's cousin's house, seeing his roommate when they met one another. The guy Beverly was there to see walked out the room, and then Beverly tried to talk to Mike; he talked about her like a dog. He told me she was acting like a "Hoe". He said to me "Some kind of friend she is to you Jean." She was only out of North East Pre-Release Center for ninety days before she returned. She had been stealing again, trying to support her drug habit. She caught another case. I really was hoping that she did not come back, but she did. Monday, 1994, the month of February, Beverly came back to the prison, and she came to my unit. She sent someone to tell me to come outside. I knew she wanted something. I started not to go because she was beginning to be a big pain in my side. I went on outside to see what she wanted, no one wanted to be worried with her because she would mess people around, and she couldn't be trusted.. She wanted some cigarettes and I said I "do not have any" she said "Jean I know you got some cigarettes"; I said "I have just enough for me until we shop next week," and I am not going to come up short. Then she asked for a cookie, "I said I do not have any pop, which I do not drink, I do not have anything. I did offer her some menthol roll-up's she did not want them. I said "You are a proud baggier pimp on." I did not want to write to my pen pal, Ron, anymore because he had become very boring. The only thing he was always talking about was sex, and freaking. He really did not have any kind of a conversation. I asked him one time if he would send me an envelope because I was low on money, and I did not see anything wrong with it if he wanted me to write him. Most men would not have had a problem with that. He said he felt that he did not have to pay for my conversation. I told him to stop writing me because I did not need a pen pal like him. I felt he was a cheap man because a stamp only was 29 cents, and if I was not worth that, then I was not worth writing. The last letter I god from him, his roommate put a letter into the envelope with Ron's letter, for me. I thought that he was a pretty cool guy; he wanted me to find him a nice lady to write to. He wanted a lady much like me. He liked my conversation. He said Ron told him I was a very intelligent and pleasing to look at from the many pictures of myself that I had sent to him. He never sent me one of himself. He probably was on state pay. I had to tell his roommate there were no other like me and I was not going to look for him someone to write because it was too time consuming for me to do.

My family members used to say I was a mean person; I got it from my mom because to me she was a very mean lady. My oldest deceased sister used to say she did not think either one of us was mean. I am the middle child out of six, and I am more like my mother than any of my siblings. I just do not like people talking "Mess" about me and lying on me, but who am I that people cannot lie on or talk about; they lied on Jesus Crist. It took me a very long time to get over people talking about me. The more I got educated the more I knew how to fight intelligently. With the Lord's help, I am getting better and overcoming different issues that come in my life today.

My other pen-pal from London prison in Ohio went home. He wanted to come and see me. I thought he was lying. He was Spanish. I did what I had to do to get him on my visiting list; I sent him a lot of pictures of me. He never sent one picture of himself. I wanted him to know what I looked like. I had no idea what he looked like. He finally came to see me. I did not know what to expect, to do or to say. I walked into the visiting hall looking all around. No one said anything to me. I told the co who was in charge that I had no idea who my visit was. She asked the visitors who were there for Doris Williams to stand up and come up to the desk. He stood up, and he was about 5' 8" tall and about 150 pounds, had wavy hair to his shoulders, with a very thick mustache. He grabbed and hugged me. He wanted to kiss me, but I turned my cheek to him and said, "Not now," because I did not know him. We went and sat down and started talking. It was a very enjoyable visit getting to know him. He was in my corner ever since he had sent me a clothes box, and he even sent me money every month. I cared for him a great deal because he did not have to like me enough to come see me or do anything for me. I told him from the first day that I did not love him, and he said that was ok. He still was going to do for me anyway.

The Lord Jesus touched me since I had to do three years behind bars. I was raised up in the church all my life; my grandfather was a preacher in Fort Wayne, Indiana. God's word had always been around me in my life; and how I had embarrassed my family. At least that is what my dead sister, the nurse, told me while she was living. I have learned to *never- say- never*. One of my mother's friends from church came to see me to talk about how God loves me in 1982 when I got home. I knew all of that; I really did not want to hear that talk from her at that time. She went on to tell me that she had told my mother years ago that I was her special child and that hurt me because I had always been so defensive, I use to think I was being threaten all the time and really did not know why I was like that and easy to get my feeling hurt. I think I have to really look into my past and ask myself why was I like

that,. I used to cry at the drop of a dime. I asked the church lady sister
Washington who is also gone home what she meant by that statement.
She said' "Jean it's nothing bad. God got his special plans for you. He
just wants you to work for Him." At the time it did not faze me at first
because I was not ready to hear that. I wanted to do the right things
in life and live right, so I got baptized again. I was always asking why
this and why that. Once a Christian person told me everything is not
always meant to know why, but me, I had always believed there was a
why behind everything a person may say, or you just do not know the
reason at that given time, but that person knows, and sometimes it is
negative thoughts. I prayed and prayed for God to open my eyes to the
known as well as to the unknown, to let me see the evil things before
they happen to me. Three months after I was locked up, one night
while in my bed I dreamed God came to me; it was the most beautiful
dream, God showed me everything. I had so many questions about Him
talking to me for the first time, and I heard and I understood Him. He
said to me "I am my mother's special child and there are great things
waiting for me. I remember when this same friend of my mother's came
back to talk to me after getting home in 1995. She spoke the same words
to me. There were so many people God was working through to try
and make me see myself. I could not see it because I was in darkness
for many, many years, and I did not know it. God has shown me that
one of my gifts is to motivate others. Mother Mary Fryer Washington
before she went home to be with the Lord told me that she had seen the
change in me. That was great news to my ears.

I was on the downside of my time now. This is one year I thought
I would never see. I have seen so many women come and leave from
this prison and come back within a few months for a new case. There
were over 600 women at North East Pre-Release Center (NEPRC). This
was a penitentiary inside the city limits. We had a lot of male guards.
There were a few I would have not mind getting to know better or even
dated, but I did not talk to them much because most of the time there
were always women in their faces: big ones, small ones, medium ones,
cute ones, and ugly ones. So I did not act like the rest of the women.

I have always wondered how male guards feel when there are so many women inmates giving them play. They are men, so I know there are some women they wish they could get with or even start a relationship with. A few guards were escorted off the compound for having a relationship or sex with an inmate. This particular inmate let the guard reach his climax in her mouth. Later, she put it in a cup and took it up to the front office, and he was out of a job. Another white shirt supervisor captain, a black man let an inmate did him wrong to lose his job; that really was a shame because he had a wife and children. How could he ever explain that situation to his wife? There were rumors that some guards let the inmates play and rub on their penises. Now that would be a thrill considering how long we women have been without a man. I think I would have been scared so much until I really could not enjoy it. It was very common for the inmates to make love to one another.

Later, we had started back taking pictures and playing bingo again. We never got the skates; I did not believe that anyway. That was inmates talking. The prison had taken pictures and bingo away from us a year before because they were talking about saving on money, and some activates had to be cut back. The prison was very confusing because we had to follow all the changes and rules. The rules seemed as though they were always changing. For example, we could wear different colored clothes. Then they wanted to take colors away from us. At first we could have white jogging suits but no white blouses because the sergeants wore white shirts, so they stopped us having anything white. Those of us who had white jogging suits had to send them home, and the money came out of the inmates' pockets. A few months later, they said we could wear white jogging suits again. Families got tired of the back and forth ideas of the prison. The color red was said that it interfered with the cameras; yet still, the past summer, we could wear red. There was some mess about the inmates who had TVs. The inmates who had them all of a sudden could not put them onto our dressers. The prison said the desktops were for writing; however, the ladies in each room worked that out. I myself and some of the other ladies put our TV in the bed with us at the foot. Some cos had something to say about that; others were fine with it. We were told that our TV goes under the bed on the floor when we were not watching it. Well, I did not want to put my TV under the bed because I had a top bunk. Then it was told to us to watch TV on top of our lock boxes. I asked them why I should have to look way down on the first bunk to see my TV. It was too far away. I left it in the bed with me. I got written up sometimes about that situation. Nothing happened when I was heard on the dumb ticket.

At this present writing, we are in the month of February 1994, I haven't heard anything from my dear husband, and I do not think I will. All of the women who left and promised to keep in touch, have not but I'm not worried about that because it is a known and proven fact that once they get outside of the gates, they do not remember any of us they left behind; very few of them do remember. It is so hard to make real friends in prison.

My roommate, Ramos, was sick all weekend; she had something like muscle spasms from what she was telling us. All she would need is muscles relaxers to ease the pain, but the prison people at NEPRC think we are lying about everything and all our illnesses; it isn't about lying all the time. She suffered all weekend. She was taken to the hospital; she came back and said they did not do anything for her. The hospital wanted to give her Motrin 800 which would not help the pain. They gave us Motrin for everything, and we would not get anything stronger, so she had to suffer with that pain until Monday when she saw the doctor, and he did not even come in until 3:00 p.m., so she was in pain, and that was a shame that we could not get decent medical attention. She saw the doctor that afternoon and he gave her a muscle relaxer and made her take it in front of him. She had made the statement that she did not want to die in prison. She ended up asking to go back to Marysville because she felt she would get better medical care there. On February 6, 1994, I finally broke down and called my husband, he was so glad to hear from me. He had informed me that he had been in and out of jail himself for the past three months; he had a case for grand theft. I asked him what he had stolen. He said a car and a big screen TV, but I asked him why he stole that stuff. He did not answer me. He had said his sister knew the people, and they called on both of them. He was on drugs because that was something he would not have done if he had not been on drugs. He also broke into the people's house, so I was thinking it was all drug related. Mike stayed in the county jail for three months because he had had a one hundred thousand dollar bond and no one was going to get him out, so he said he was in the psych ward. Drugs had probably fried his brains he used to tell me things and I never heard so much ridiculous stuff in my life. He had been living with his mother for the two years while I had been in prison. He told me he was doing sub-contracting which I did not believe him. He said when I get out he would have somewhere for me to stay which I did not believe that either. If he did or did not, I really did not care anymore because my feeling for him was not the same, and I never got back with him until 2015. I still loved and cared about him, but I am no longer in love with him, and he will always be my friend if he wants to be friends. However, if not, then there is no love lost. I will always wish him the best in life because of the road he was taking and what he and I had been through in life. I knew he would be locked up like me. He caught a case, and he told me that his lawyer said he had a very good chance of getting probation because he really did not have a bad record, and the fact that he gave the television back, but we will see what happens to him. He did do six months in the work house for another case. He was saying that he was about to go into a rehabilitation center for six months. Mike was a big liar; at least he used to be. I asked him why was he doing that, when he is going to get out and do the same thing which is use of drugs. He said that he was not using. I did not believe that because he stayed in trouble. I told him if he was not using, like the judge told me, rehabilitations is for users. He went for sentencing for his grand theft case on February 28, 1994. May God may have mercy on his soul.

One of my old roommates is back. She came and found me in the laundry room. When I looked up and saw her face, I jumped off the dryer where I was sitting at the time, and I gave her a big hug. It was good to see her but not under those circumstances. She had not been gone from NEPRC for a good six months.

They made an honor unit at NEPRC, and I wanted to go to it. I had to put in a pass what was called a kite to my unit manager explaining why I felt I should be in the honor unit. The qualifications were the inmate had to be at NEPRC for a year or more with no laydowns meaning hole time. I was thinking the hole was like a hole in the ground. When an inmate goes to the hold she cannot have anything but her lotion, hair grease, a comb, tooth brush, tooth paste, a change of stocks, underwear, something to read, writing materials, bed liners, towels, and soap. There was only one bed in the hole cell per inmate; the bed sat 12 inches off the floor with two very thin mattresses on it. Inmates also must be of medium statue. I fitted the description. I got my girlfriend Cherrie, and I into the honor dorm because she did not know how to write that well. We moved in on that Friday February, 18, 1994. By being in the honor unit we got to have a little more privileges such as we got to order food out twice a month from Mr. Hero, chicken or pizza. In addition, instead of us getting four visits a month we got five. Instead of spending $50 at the commissary, we could spend $60, and we could stay up twenty-four hours, seven days a week if we wanted to, but during the week we had to stay on the second floor because they did not want us wondering around downstairs on the first floor. Everything was downstairs--the telephone, the ice, hot water, and the microwave. We still had to also get up and go to work the next morning. No one really stayed up twenty-four hours during the week. Being in the honor unit were only forty inmates to deal with instead of ninety. To me, that was a big difference. The co's expected us to be quiet somewhat which was almost impossible for us to maintain the amount of noise because so much steel was around us--the seats, the chairs, the tables, the beds, the rails, etc. We all were on the second floor; there were no bedrooms on the first floor in the honor unit.

Mr. Walker was one of my favorite co's when I got out; I would not have minded hooking up with him on the streets. He would never tell me his first name. Maybe that was against the rules for the co's to share that information with the inmates. Mr. Walker gave me a few ideas about this book as I was writing it in prison. I appreciated all of his input because he really did have some very good ideas, and hopefully one day I will be able to go out on a date with him and just "Kick it.

An inmate called home and got some very bad news from her

mother the day I am writing this. All a sudden there was a very loud holler. Then inmates got up and went over to see what had happened. She had gone to the floor, balled up in a fetal position crying and hollering saying, "No, no, why?" At that point no one knew what had happened. I thought she had fallen down the stairs or something at first, but then I saw the telephone just hanging off the hook, and her telephone book and other papers were scattered all over the floor. One inmate went and picked her stuff up off of the floor and started talking to the person on the other end of the telephone which was her mother, and she said someone was in a car accident and died, the woman said, "Tell her to call back later tonight after she calms down." Everyone in the unit was crying. After we had her calmed down enough to call back home to find out details about what exactly had happened. She was too upset at the time to talk about what had happened. The Chaplain took her to his office to talk to her to give her some encouraging words. She and I were roommates until she got her single room. She and I were pretty "Cool." I came to find out that her middle brother, aunt, and a cousin were in a car accident and died; it was said that they had died instantly. My mouth fell open; I could not do anything else but hug her. She could not attend the funeral services because they were out of state in Atlanta, Georgia. When a tragedy such as what Star went through regardless where the funeral is at the inmate should be able to go at the expense of the family. My time was getting short. I thought I would never see it to that day; my time was looking really good. I had *eleven months and counting down.* When I first got locked up, I could not see that much time. I was surely counting down. The worst was definitely behind me.

Mom was trying to come and see me in the heart of the winter months when the weather was really bad; I told her that I was fine and not to be worrying trying to come down to see me. When the weather got better, I told her around April and she then started coming back to see me. She came to see me at least once a month. She and I did not argue.

I had not talked to my husband since he went to court; he tried in no way to get in touch with me. I figured if he had gotten some time his people would at least took my letters to him or re mailed them because I wrote and wrote him and never got an answer. I did not know what to think. As I was talking to Beverly about him, she kept telling me to call him and find out what had happened, I said, "Why should I when he do not give a damn about me, I had been locked up for two years, he has given me no support." I knew it was over between him and I. One day in May I broke down and called him. Months had passed since he went to court. When the call was made to him, I heard him answer the telephone. He did not know I could hear him. The telephone went dead to see if the charges would be accepted. He did accept the charges. At first he acted like he was glad to hear from me until I started fussing about what he had not been doing for me. I told him when I got out I was going to file for a divorce. He said that he had already done that and I should have my papers in a few days because he was going to get married again. I told him that was great news, but I know Mike lie to make himself look good. He was really being a dog like I had heard about other men divorcing their woman while in jail or the other way around. I think that is so low of a person to do.

As of August 2, 1994, I had not gotten any divorce papers. I finally got around to asking him about his case. I told him I did not want to keep fussing with him about his case. He finally told me he came out with three years' probation, which I feel that is set-up for failure. He is the only person I know who keeps getting out of trouble over and over again. One of these times the judge is going to slam dunk him with some real time. He had the nerve to tell me that him and his new woman stopped at my sister and brother-in- law's house; he had not been at their house the whole time I had been locked up which was two years. I told him he had a lot of nerve to take his new woman to my sister's house. That was the last time I talked to him, and I have no intentions of calling him back ever again. As far as I am concerned, he is out of my life completely now and forever.

I had to call my sister in Cleveland because I was very curious if Mike and his woman had been to my sister's house or not; sure enough, my sister said he and her had stopped by one evening. Mike pulled into the drive way. My brother in-law went outside and saw him. He had a much older woman than he was in the car who he introduced as his woman, My sister said she did not even go outside to meet her, and he was not about to bring her into the house.

You would be surprised how many people are in prison who are said to be innocent, like this one inmate. She was another one who's at NEPRC got sentenced to life and has been locked up now for twenty years as of this writing. She and another inmate tried to escape. It was said that both of them were found in the ghetto not too far from the prison, NEPRC. I do not know if they knew someone over there or if they had made plans with someone and someone must have gotten tired of them and reported them. One received another five to fifteen years on her life sentence, yet the white girl who was with her received six months. What kind of mess was that? I did not understand it at all. Where is the justice? At this time I am thinking about going back to college when I get out studying drug counseling or x-ray technology.

My sister, Ola, from Atlanta, Georgia, came to town May 24 to visit Mom and the family and they came down to see me on Friday May 27, 1994.She looked really good. She had just gotten married; she had picked up a lot of weight. I told her I did not know who was worse, she or I because I've always been a "yo-yo" with my weight. I had a very nice visit with my family. I asked Ola to let me see her wedding ring; it was about a two carat, and.diamonds were all over the ring, then she too had one big diamond in the middle; it was just gorgeous.

One of my pen-pals, who I was writing, made cards in Grafton; they are really nice cards-- nude women on them for birthdays, anniversaries. Anything a person wants, it can be ordered; you name it; he made it. The cards even have fancy writing inside, nothing like the cards the women make at NEPRC because we do not get the equipment. The men get to do things like that. He told me he sold the cards to the men in prison with him and makes a killing. That's one of his hustler activities. He started sending me cards to help me make some money, and the women wanted to know how I got those kinds of pictures in. Then I said the mail had to let them through I guess. The cards sold very well, especially the nude women because the women love to send those cards out to their men on the street. My pin pale was sending me anywhere between three and fifteen cards a week. Each card I sold for a pack of cigarettes or equal to whatever I wanted at the store, and the cards that were personalized were 50 cent more. The women did not mind paying what I asked for the cards because they were getting what they wanted. The cards were quantity and quality work; he could not send me enough materials because as soon as I got them, they were gone. The women were looking for me to see what kind of cards I had. I could not emphasize enough how much he helped me while I was locked up, he still thought about helping me. He made my last eleven months very much enjoyable. I did not have to smoke rolled-up cigarettes, thanks to him I was smoking name brand cigarettes.

My dear, so called friend, Beverly, had left me again, but this time I was right behind her. She left on July 8, 1994. We stayed together all that day. She was not there to celebrate the 4th of July with us because we did not celebrate it until July 19th, which was called yard day for us. She left prison weighing 160 pounds. When she left the first time, she weighed 210 pounds. She had lost a lot of weight because she was on the stem fast smoking Crack-Cocaine. She was looking well with the weight off of her. I used to try to talk to her all the time about her changing her ways. I told her she should try to get her GED, to take up a trade or something, yet she still used to try to fool people in thinking she had graduate from high school. She was only fooling herself. I think at least she realized who her friends really were and who was in her corner and meant her well. I talked about her badly enough hoping some of it stayed with her when she walked back out and hit the streets. She stated she was going to go to a NA meeting to get to know those people and try to hang with and around a different crowd of people. I told her that is what she needed; she had said she was not going to start hanging with those same people she was with before because now she saw they did not mean her any good. She saw when she was locked up the first and second times that none of those so called friends were there for her. I told her it was time to open her eyes. She had to start looking around her, looking at her life being wasted whereby she would have nobody trusting and wanting to be around her under the circumstances. She was trying to get her life together. She left me again. I had another eleven months. I told her to come on back a third time to watch me leave her here. She said she was not coming back this time. I said, "I have heard that before. " She said again that she was going to send me a piece of money. "Girl," I said, "you need to just stop lying because you think of no one but yourself." She said she was going to keep her word this time. I told her that her word is not anything to me and that it did not mean anything to me anymore. She said now she understood how bad she hurt me, and I was the only friend she had. I knew that. I could always see things in other people, but I could not see my own. I was so good at giving others the right advice but could not give myself the right things to do and the right people to be around at the time. It took me a very long time to learn. Therefore, God had put on my heart and in my mind to be a social worker a very long time ago. Now I am following through with God's work. I told Beverly if she did not keep her word this time, when I got out I was going to be finish with her, and she knew that I meant that. She made me fill out a blank envelope to send the money back to me in a family member's name. I felt in my heart she was going to do the right thing this time by me when she left.

When we got mail that following Tuesday after Beverly left, sure enough there was my envelope I had filled out for her with a money stamp on the envelope. I just smiled and said, "I just hope and pray she stays away from that crack and does something with her life." I saw a long time ago that I made impacts on people's lives, and I really did not know what I was doing at the time but being me, and I was doing God's work all the time and I did not even know it. The seed was planted a very long time ago. I can say that Beverly kept her word; she had a heart and saw just how close she and I really were.

She has two beautiful children she needed to be taking care of. Her daughter was a teenager and needed her. Her son was only twelve and growing up. He is a sweetheart. He captures my heart because he is a very minable little boy who really looks out for his crazy ass mother. I did not know if Beverly went to the NA meeting or not, but I hope she stay out of trouble and stays out of the stories stealing. I never heard from her again.

This was really a good year for me because my brothers and sisters came home that year, and no doubt they wanted to see me. My brother who is under me in age is home from Nova-Scotia Canada; he and his two sons, they were in Cleveland July, 15, 1994. I was really impressed at my brother's appearance; he stands 6'-6" tall, he wore his hair long in a Jerry Curl, and it is pass his shoulders. All the inmates were asking me who he was. Then they wanted me to hook them up with him. My brother was not interested in any of them. Some of the inmates told me to tell him that they would wrap their legs around his neck any day. I had him cracking up at some of the things the ladies were telling me to tell him; this one lady wanted him to wait on her until 1996 when she got out to meet him. I told him what she had said, and he said he do not going to wait that long for anyone to get out of jail, especially when he did not know her.

Yard day that year was on July 19th basically it was the same as previous years. I think we had better food, more games, better prizes, and the ice cream was better by giving us Butter Pecan, my favorite ice cream. We could get as much as we wanted. I helped serve the ice cream. I ate so much ice cream that I did not want to see any more for a few weeks.

I had been in the honor unit six months. It had its advantages as well as disadvantages. I got new roommates one day who were Carrie, Teresa, and Alice. Alice slept under Teresa, I sleep on top of Carrie, Teresa and Carrie was white. Alice and I are African American. We all got along ok most of the time. Carrie weighed about three hundred pounds; I hated sleeping over her because she shook me getting in and out of the bed. She could not get out of the bed without holding the rail that was on the top of her bed, and it was under my bed. Whenever she was in the bed, I really could not rest or sleep. I tossed and turned all night. When she would get out the bed in the morning, I would wake up because the bed shook so badly. She used to make a lot of noise getting dressed in the morning going to work. She breathed very hard like she was tired all the time. Maybe that was her weight. It was too much weight on her, and she was not trying to lose a pound. She ate all the time, and she was getting bigger. She was one of the sweetest persons you ever want to meet although she was fat. She had a sense of humor and was a very fun and smart person to be around. Alice was the youngest in the room, she was a cool person, however, she was a dyke, if that was what she preferred a women, then that was her business as long as she did not come at me we did not have any problems. Sometimes she would over reacted on things and bent the truth a lot. I think she did that because she had a very ruff childhood, but so did I. She had been locked up for nine years; she did not really have the support from her family. Her family never came to see her. Alice lived on state pay and got no food or clothes boxes like everyone else. I felt so sorry for her. At the time of this writing, the six months I have been her roommate, she has had no visits. She used to tell me all the time that she saw so many wonderful and beautiful qualities in me. She always talked very highly of me, and I tried to always give her the best advice I could possible give. Alice shared a lot of things with me, and I helped her whenever I could. Everyone in the honor dorm had at least been locked up for two years or better. As it stood, I will be the first to be leaving the room to go home.

Finally, for the first time I saw my pen pal, Johnnie, every Tuesday. The c o's took twelve to thirteen ladies to Grafton institution to the dentist; that was where he was,. I had told him I was coming, but I did not know when, so I was trying to find out beforehand in enough time to write and tell him so he could come to the dentist's office to see me. I did not find out in time to let him know. I was hurt. As my name was called to see the dentist, I was walking down the hall with the c o and got so close to the male guard sitting at the door with the other men, and I saw this other really tall man standing there. He was an inmate. He was Johnnie. As I got closer to him, he and I just locked eyes. I gave him a big, big smile, and nodded my head at him. He did not take his eyes off of me for one second; that was such a very good feeling. He looked long and deep at me as if I had no clothes on. We watched each other until we got out of each other's eyesight. I wanted so badly to say something to him, and he wanted to say something to me as well, but we were instructed not to talk to the men, and they could not talk to us; all we could do was look. We knew each other by our pictures. He looked just like his pictures. I was so happy the rest of that day because

I felt I had finally seen my future husband so I thought, and I wanted so badly to hear his voice and I could not.

When I got back to NEPRC that evening, I sat down and wrote him a letter, telling him that was a big surprise for me to see him standing there waiting for me to come out, and how in the world he knew I was on that ride? He said they get the names of the ladies who that are on the ride every week. He happened to ask the c.o if he could see the sheet that Tuesday, and he saw my name. He said he had to come there to see me. His impression was that I was a very beautiful person and that my beauty shows in my letters. He may have not been the best- looking man I have had, but he was to me moderately handsome, plus I knew I'll have a solid foundation with him. So by us seeing each other for the first time did us both all the good in the world.

Mom had to go to the hospital because her ulcer had flared up. At first she did not want to go as usually. Luckily, my baby sister was at the house, and mom kept on blacking out. My sister had to get her dressed and made her go to the hospital. Once she was there, they kept her. She needed a blood transfusion. She stayed in intensive care for three days. She was in one of the best hospitals we have in Cleveland which was Marymount. She went home a week later. My father had a stroke and did not know it; he told my mother he could not walk. My mother knew he had had a stroke. She looked at his mouth, and it was twisted. Even then he still did not want to go to the hospital. He knew one of the times in the hospital that he was not going to come out alive. Mom had to make him go to the hospital, and they kept him for two days. My dad was paralyzed on his left side. I told him that it was a good thing he was right- handed. He could not walk up the steps by himself. Although he had a cane, he did not fully know how to use it yet. Mom had said he could use his left hand a little. He still tried to wash dishes. In the process he was about to fall. He had lost his balance a little bit and tried to put his weight on his left side. He had to remember to put all his weight on his right side and when going up the steps, he had to remember to step with his right leg first, then his left, instead of leading off with his left first. He tried to walk regularly up the steps but could not. In due time, when he got used to not having hardly any use of his left side, he was alright. I told my sister I could not take too much of my family members health failing on me while I am still locked up all this happen in 1994 and there was nothing I could do..

The prison started this new release whereby when an inmate who was doing flat time got down to two hundred days left on her sentence; she could file for an early release. If this was granted, an inmate had the chance of leaving early. Since I was doing flat time and met all of the qualifications, I got a chance of being released early around February or March of 1995 instead of July. I really needed to be at home with my parents because they both needed someone at the house with them. What I did not know about the early release was that they took your good days; some kind of way it would not have worked out for me. Therefore, I did not apply for the early release.

My oldest sister from Georgia had just gotten married a while ago. I was sad that I could not be in the wedding or I could not have been there because I was locked up. She came home again on August 4, 1994, and she brought her new husband with her so I could meet him. I was so excited that my sister brought my new brother-in-law to see me. I had a special visit set up for them for Thursday August 11, 1994. They stayed just about all day. My mother and niece came with them. My brother-in-law has the most beautiful eyes you ever wanted to see. They were a light brown. I had to ask him if he had on contacts. He said, "No." He and I got to know each other a little. My sister let me sit next to him because she knew I was going to ask him a thousand questions because my sister was very independent, and she was the head RN nurse at her hospital in Atlanta, Georgia, which was at Crawford Long. He said my two sisters and I have big legs. We got them from Mom. Then mom said she got her big legs from *her* mother who we called Dear, my grandmother. I told my new brother- in- law at the end of our visit that I think we will keep him in the family. He smiled. I think he and my sister made a good couple. They acted as if they really were in love, although he was a lot younger than her. My sister said he was a funny eater. He ate a lot of junk food. She also said he likes a plain burger. He said cheese was no good; however, he would take ketchup and mustard on his burger. I said "I am not going to talk about him because I am a funny eater myself". We started a conversation on talking about old times back in the day. I told him when we were children; I could not stand my sister Ola because she never wanted to play with my brother and I to tear the house up when Mom and Dad had gone to work. Mostly this was in the summer months. She was always the good one who wanted to play Mommy. She said one time that I made her so angry that she pushed me down the steps and knocked all of my teeth out of my mouth. She said I was a tomboy, which was so true. I did not remember that incident, but my mother was sitting there, and she said that was true. I asked if she had gotten a beating because Mom never beat her, she said she "Got the living mess beat out of her." Mom said, "Yes, I tore her buttock up." I did not remember too many times that Ola got a whooping. I remember when she scratched my face really badly. My mother was not home. When she did come home, the only thing she did to her was make her cut all her finger nails off, and I mean they were very long. Afterwards, they were super short. She was hurt for months. I think she cried for weeks.

At the time of this writing, one of my friends, Cherrie goes home in four days, August 19. I will be so glad for her to go home; I called her "Fatal attraction" because that is what she was. She said that "She came from the kind of family that got drunk and wanted to fight or cry." She used to tell me all the time that her breasts made her big money. I believed that because she had some big old "Tits." She was also a hooker, "a lady of the night." She did not have any kind of education what so-ever; no one in her family had either. Her sister, Joan, was locked up with us for a short period of time. I used to love hearing them say words that they could not pronounce. Joan said their oldest sister was on her way to the prison. It would be hell to tell the captain. With three sisters, that would have been a big mess. Linda is her name, she had only six months, and she ran, so the police was looking for her. That is one family that I would not like being around. On the other hand every family has sick members in their family and I was one of them.

There were a lot of women at NEPRC for a lot of different reasons; I've seen women on death row, women who were doing life for one reason or the other. There were a lot of things I could understand, but a baby killer; I have no understanding of that. Why would anyone want to hurt an innocent little baby? People with violent crimes like baby killers should never get out of prison. There were also people who had harmed and killed elderly people for whatever reason. Money is the cause usually. People like that cannot defend themselves; a lot of the killing were for drugs or because they would not give their money up to the inmate, or just maybe the elderly person was trying to protect him or herself. An inmate did a few years or so and went to the board, and she really thought the board "Should have cut her loose." The inmate should have gotten two or three more years slapped on him or her to shock him or her back into reality. I feel violent criminals should be locked up and the key thrown away.

In prison there are all kind of women, and all kind of nationalities with different attitudes to deal with. I feel the inmates should be separated, the inmates in the following catalog all murders, and baby killers should be put or house together, all thefts together, drug traffics, and drug user together, hookers, and hoes in the same housing unit, all minors together, and all rapist together. I feel the prison should not mix all the inmates together like they do because some people come into the penitentiary for the first time in their life, some come at a young age, others come at a late age, regardless of the fact they are scared, and it might not be that they are hard core criminal. They made a mistake, maybe more than once. I feel the institution should not throw them all together because they are not street people, who are very street smart, and the cons people who think they are so smart, but there is always someone just a little bit smarter. If they were so smart, they would not be in the penitentiary. Then there are the ones who think they are big and bad people, really they are not because there is always someone a little bigger and balder than them. A lot of inmates be scared of this kind of acting, or they learn more wrong stuff and slickness in prison. I know it was all kind of slick stuff brought my way, and I told them all they were crazy. When you find this kind of women, she does whatever somebody else tells her to do unless she is a very strong person, there are inmates who protects, however, the time the protector wants her for herself. Yes, that happen to me, but I was too strong minded to go there.

These ladies I called them maids because they iron, wash, give them her money or buy her things at the commissary, cleaning and or anything else that the protector might want her to do. I did not think this kind of caring on was right, and then who was I to speak on anything.

There were inmates, who wanted to better themselves by going to college or even getting their GED these people should also be separated from the general population. I have saw inmates locked up for five years or better and did not even make an attempt to get their GED, but it was said she will do things when she gets back on the street. If she did not do it while God sat down for a while, it will be very hard for her to do anything when she gets out. Some of these women go in front of the board after pulling about four, five years or so, and they did not make an attempt to accomplished their GED, they were only letting the board members know they did not want to do anything in life but the same thing that brought them to prison in the first place.

I had enrolled in college at the time I did not know what I wanted or what I wanted to do in life; I did not really know how important a college education and gaining knowledge was. I thought being slick and hanging with the bad crowd was happening; I was so wrong. I would have enrolled sooner than what I did listening to inmates that do not really know what they were talking about misguided me concerning my future in my studying. The prison is full of hater and devil people. Because I had an outstanding loan that I was in default with the federal government, I thought I would not be entitled to continue college until that matter was paid off. I did not attempt to fill out the grant papers to see if I would be accepted or rejected; I just threw away three years, not really because I was writing those three years. I decided to fill the paperwork out anyway; the inmates started scaring me saying things like if I did get the grant and the institution found out, I was in default of the loan, and I would have another case, I did not need that kind of trouble, but I wanted to go back to school, I got my federal grant back, which it did get denied for the payment of books, however, I did get the state grant which paid my tuition. I was ready to start classes in the winter on 1995 at the prison we started three weeks late; this was time we had to make up before the quarter was over. My goal was to make the dean's list. I knew it would mean that I'd had to constantly study.

The quarter was not quiet half way over, it was time for midterms, I thought I'd do better on my psychology test than sociology test because I had studied psychology more and spent more time on it than I did on sociology. I found psychology very hard. I had to take more psychology and philosophy during my education. So I really wanted to learn the material well, also psychology interested me because it explained why people behave as they do and the mental processes involved. Just as I figured we had received are midterm papers back, in sociology I knew that I could do it. I received an A in psychology and a B in sociology. At times, I did find that psychology and sociology are very much alike. I've even found that the same words were in both books, however, there were different meanings. It was confusing at times, but I had to remember that psychology was the study of the human mind and its functions, especially the behavior and sociology was the study of society social lives of people, groups, and societies and the study of etc. They both are very interesting subjects.

If I could have kept the motivation, and ambition about college, I just might make it. Learning is fun and I can accomplish the things in life that I want. My psychology teacher once told me that if I continue telling myself that I cannot learn a particular thing, I won't learn, therefore, I turned it around and kept telling myself that I can and I will learn the material, and I did learn. English was my favorite subject because I knew that I had problems writing and using words correctly. I talked to my English teacher about many problems in which I had in the past. After our conversation, the teacher gave me a few names of people to contact once I got out back into society to help me with my college classes. She also shared with me that she had seen many students who did not make it through college. She said Doris, "I believe you're going to make it." That statement gave me all the confidence in the world. At times, I need to hear things like that. I needed that reassurance to confirm what I already knew because I had very low self-seemed. Compliments helped me feel that I would accomplish something that I was not hearing at home. I knew and understood that the main point was not to give up, no matter how hard it got. My reward would come in the end.

The night of August 16, 2014, I had a very weird dream about an inmate who was here, but she is gone home now, she and I was friends, in my dream some women detectives, came to my house, I was living with my mother at the time, these detectives started accusing me of stealing clothes, that my so called friend had said that I did; well, I knew nothing about this; I had just gotten home about a week; she had given these detectives my address and said I was in on this case with her. That was a big fate lie. I had not seen or been around her since I got out of prison. What she did not know was the alleged date of the crime, I still was locked up, and the two women detectives did not believe me of course. The women did not even want to see my release papers to show I was still in prison at the time of the crime. They just wanted to assume that I was a part of this crime because my friend has said so, and why did they believe her, I did not know. That dream told me to watch myself when I did get out because people are snakes; and they want to see failure. I had blouses and some pants on the couch, they saw them, which those items weren't even new, and I had just ironed them. One of the detectives picked up a blouse and said this is about a 36, she tried it on over her clothes, and said she could fit it and that's the size of the clothes and blouses that was stolen a 18 I asked, and asked them, why are you all messing with me? I have been here is this house every day since I've been out. My mother and father told them the same thing; my parents were people who would not tell a lie for anybody fear of getting in trouble. The only time I had been out of the house, I was with my mother or my boyfriend. There was no way, I could have been part of that theft that she had gotten involved in. They were not listening to anybody; they never answered any of my questions. I got sick and tired of that one detective messing with my clothes, I grabbed her and put her into a head lock that she could not get out of, I told her and her partner to get out my mother house and leave me along unless they had proof of the charges to leave me along because I could prove that I was still locked up at the time; then I woke up. I do not even want to be around anyone who gets high. I will be around my church people and people who are going in the same direction as I and that is up

At first, when I got locked up I tried not to call home too much, but after my mother and father had been in the hospital, I tried to call home at least every other week or so. Mom had been on my mind, so I called home Friday, August 26, about 8 p.m. My call was not accepted. I could only make collect calls, but usually when my call did not get accepted, my mother was not at home so I just figured she had gone over to my sister's house. I got up Saturday morning and called home again because she still was on my mind. I called again about 10 am that morning. She answered the phone.

Mom said she did not feel too well which was on that Friday. That morning she said she went to yawn and her mouth got stuck open. She could not close her mouth. It scared her. My brother was up on the third floor at the time, so she started beating on the wall until she got his attention, and he went downstairs to see what was going on. She was trying to tell my father that she could not close her mouth, but he did not understand her. They were asking her what was wrong. There was no sound coming out of her mouth. My brother ran across the street to get my mother's friend who was a nurse. She went over and did what she could to help. Mom stayed like that for two hours. She said it was a very hurting feeling and she did not want to experience that anymore. I told her from then on when she yawned not to open her mouth so widely. She started to go to the hospital, but she did not because she was looking at the cost. I told her if I had of been home, she would have gone to the hospital because I would have taken her whether she wanted to go or not. She started talking about how much money she owed the hospital from when she and my father were in the hospital before. I told her no money can buy their health and their health comes before any bill because bills are going to be around when they are dead and gone. She said, "Yeah, Jean, your right." My mother had said my sister Ola in Georgia who also was a nurse had called home that Saturday morning which she usually did once a week to see how she and Dad were doing. Ola told Mom the same thing that I had told her about not opening her mouth so widely.

As the holidays passed, the first of the year approached *January 1, 1995.* I thought I would never make it to see the day my name appeared on the furlough board list. It was the first time, after 2 ½ years that my name appeared on something that had to do with my freedom. The board was to meet on January 18, 2015. I brought the new years in on my knees, praying and thanking God for keeping me safe, giving me knowledge, directing me toward a career and opening my eyes, realizing that prison is not for me. The school quarter had ended. I did very good, I wanted to continued college when I got out.

It was time for all college students to get re-classed to new jobs. I was supposed to work for Lieutenant Williams as his clerk. I was waiting for him to arrange for me to take a typing test he kept on giving me the run around he was full of mess just like I had heard. I was re-classed in two days to a second shift porter in my unit. I thought that they could give the college students better jobs than that. To me, that's a form of punishment or a job for new arrivals at NEPRC. Some ladies were put back in CFS the kitchen. So, I should have been happy. I am on my way home and I refused to let anything or anybody upset me because I did not have long before I'll be home.

We had finals at first my psychology and sociology teacher was talking about taking us into the middle of January to make up the time we had missed in the beginning of the quarter. The staff started questioning the instructor about our grades because all other classes were finished and grades were turned in. By having the same teacher for both my classes I was better prepared for finals; because I was familiar with her testing style. She gave us a take home final exam with four psychology questions and four sociology questions. Take home exams are always more in depth than a test in the class room; however, I have always like take home exams because I always do better on them. One of the questions was to explain Freud's theory of psychology. In sociology, one of the questions was to explain and give examples of Pavlov's experiences with conditioning his dog. I tried to be very descriptive and detailed with my explanations. Even though it was a short exam, I wanted to accomplish more than what she expected. I gave definitions of words that I used as I wrote; both my papers were 28 and

29 pages long hand written.. I was the only one in both classes to write that much. One student even commented, and said Doris "You did a lot of work and writing that the teacher did not want. " Who was she to tell me what or what not the teacher wanted? She "did her paper the way she wanted too, and I did my paper as I wanted too.

It's never too late, I'm glad and I thank "God that he has finally shown me the right way, "I finally acknowledge and accept the right way of life. I am a very stubborn person. If I never made the dean's list again, I can say that I did accomplish that goal and made it that one time. I hope and pray I'll be able to continue doing this good while in college, I can only continue doing my best at all times.

As the parole board date approached, everyone was on pins and needles. I was not because I knew and felt in my heart that the parole board would give me my furlough. Besides, God had showed me that I was going home. I only had two to three months left anyway. My time was finally approaching. My out date was July 1, 2015, my furlough if granted, I would go home about two months earlier with restrictions. I was not afraid to go in front of the furlough board, at this point, I had no idea what I would say at my furlough hearing. One thing for certain, it was something that would not be rehearsed, I'd asked God to let me open my mouth and let the proper words come out as He wanted me to say them. For me this was just another day. I wanted it confirmed that I would be leaving NEPRC, and going to new grounds, a step closer to home.

The board was finally over; I had to sit around all day because the regular board met first. Then the furlough board met after that. Finally, I got a call at 2:00 p.m. By 2:35 p.m., I was sitting in front of the parole board. Since I was going for a furlough, the board only consisted of one man. I went into the room, spoke to him, and I had a seat at the desk after he told me where to sit at. The first thing he said was, "We cannot make a decision today on your furlough because your PSI report isn't here, so you're going to have you to come back in May." I said, "Sir there is no reason to bring me back in May when I go home on July 1, 1995" with no paper, no nothing." He said that I had a po.int and he could not bring me back in front of the board any sooner. He put on the record that I refused my furlough. I was a little upset, but after all I had sat almost three years.

I felt it was so unfair when ladies go to the board month after month for their parole or furlough, and their (pre-sentencing investigation) reports; PSI's aren't in their files either. I was told that the county has so many reports to do that they just do not have enough man power to get around to everyone in time.

The counties should be more accurate and efficient so that when the ladies/inmates go to the board; their paperwork is at the institution in enough time. I wonder if the men go through with what the ladies go through. Since I knew I had five (5) more months before I went home; I was trying to get back into shape and lose some weight. I gained so much weight. When I came into this institution 2 1/2 half years ago, I weighed 40 pounds. I weighed 201 pounds a few months before leaving prison. All the weight on me was disgusting to me. I could not stand myself, so I tried to work on the problem. I worked out then three times a week. The first day I went I worked out hard. The next day I was so sore I couldn't hardly walk, especially walk up and down the stairs. It hurt so badly I told the workout instructor and she told me that it was natural and for me to come back to work out again. I did but I could not do that much because I was so sore. The following day I was not as sore and felt much better. My soreness was almost gone. I decided to keep working out.

My mom told me and she kept reminding me that I would not be able to wear any of my clothes when I got home. Well, I knew that. After working out for two weeks, three days a week, I could not do the entire routine since I could not jump around for an hour. However, I did not stop. When I could not do anymore I just kept on moving. I was not sore anymore, but neither did I see where I was losing any weight. My last five months seemed to be the hardest and longest for me.

Since my pen-pal had gotten me into the card business, it was hard for me to keep up with the business, the demands for the homemade cards that I made; I started to make them on my own. I would use colored construction paper and put a nice picture on the front. Sometimes, I used nude pictures which sold the best; when I could find them. I used some nice wording that I made copies of on the word processor. I covered the cards with clear plastic that my girl in the library got for me for a small price. The cards sold like hotcakes fresh off the grill. I sold each card for a pack of cigarettes which was $2.00. Depending on the size of the card and the picture it could be worth up to three packs. The ladies did not mind paying the price for what they wanted, especially the nude shots. The cards that had explicit sex were very popular such as the cards with the pictures of a penis at the lips of a Vagina. Since everyone in my unit knew that I made cards plus I had a stock of cigarettes, coffee, and other necessities, they were constantly bringing me things like glue, clear plastic, construction paper, and etc. The ladies knew I could always use those things, and I knew they would be looking for something in return. They were not doing it for free. I sometimes would offer the inmates ten cigarettes or some coffee since that's what they were looking for. Besides, I felt guilty if I did not give them something. They helped to keep me in business. I owned it all to my pen pal for starting me off in business with the sale of the cards.

Three more months, yes, I was counting down until the time I walked out of prison. The madness was just about over for me in the hell holes of NEPRC. The correction officers just changed unit assignments. They changed every three months. We were assigned a new c.o. The inmates said that he liked writing tickets. He also thought that the honor building occupants thought they were all that and were superior to the general population although we did not think that at all. We just got a few more privileges. The c.o acted as if he did not like use we had to put up with his bullshit until the middle of June. He gave me a ticket for not being up and dressed in the morning by 8:30. I had explained to him that I did not sleep at night and I did not usually go to bed until four or five o'clock in the morning. This was something I had been doing for almost a year. Old habits are difficult to break, but I had to try. If I had gotten two more tickets, I would have been thrown out of the honor unit and put back into general population, and I really did not want that. I would have had to put up with all the ladies, all the noise, and all the madness. I did not want that. I wanted to leave the prison from the honor unit because I would not have to walk all over the camp to let everyone see me leave. More and more ladies were going home from the honor building every month. There were about fifteen empty beds. They filled them with inmates from the population who had been waiting to get into the honor unit. It became so noisy in our little house. The unit only held forty women. To all of the old-timers, it was loud. We could hardly hear ourselves on the phone or hear the TV anymore. I said "Oh boy, things are changing." It was really time to go. The old inmates told the new women that it was not loud like that until they came in.

It was Easter. Since the ladies had done a good job on keeping the unit clean, our unit manager decided to let us order chicken dinners. We were supposed to eat chicken on April 4th. When one or two of the ladies who had just moved in went out into general population and ran their mouths about the chicken, it was taken away from us because that was one of the rules, and the old ladies new better to talk about it. This one inmate who weighed about three- to- four hundred pounds thought that it was not fair, so she ran up to the administration building to complain. That was the advantage we had for being in the honor dorm. Our unit manager did not tell us there was a problem of some kind; he let us think that we still were getting the chicken for dinner between 6:00 and 6:30 p.m. From an inmate we heard that we were not getting the chicken. This was very wrong and unfair to our unit. It did not matter if the inmate was new or old; the extra food was not to be talked about. We did eat Kenny King's a week later.

Four weeks away from leaving and counting, thank God. The madness was just about over for me; I would go to another level of my life. Every little thing was getting on my nerves, by this time. The least little thing that an inmate might say about the rules and regulations perturbed me. I was tired and definitely ready to go home. One of my roommates even said that she noticed my moods changing. I told her that I just did not want to be bothered; I stayed to myself, in my Bible and in my own world, trying to shut North East Pre-Release out my mind, and the entire stabbing jealous woman who are at NEPRC. When I did leave, I left all the bull and fake people there behind the gates at NEPRC. I had been hearing about how bad it had gotten on the streets. I was hearing things like, "You could go around the corner and get hit by a bullet; a person could be at the wrong place at the wrong time. However, I did not fear those things, and I did not feed into their negativity.

I had started sending some of my books, clothes, and personal items home; this way when I walked out through the gate, I'd only have one very small box to carry. I sent my television home around the middle of June. This time, I was not that close to anyone to leave it to. I would be walking out of here on June 30, 1995, home in time for the 4th of July.

The ladies there were so petty that they would steal anything that they thought would benefit them. I finally discovered that someone had stolen all of my words that I was using for my cards. Everyone knew that I was making a killing on selling all kinds of cards, and I had words beyond their imagination. Everyone wanted a piece of what I was doing. I did think that it was my roommates who stole the words. It had to be one of them because no one else could get that close to me.

My pen-pal who sent me these beautiful words that I would make copies of on the word processor to put inside of the cards. I always had a hard written original that I kept for my records. That was when I finally discovered that every last one of my word sayings were gone. I felt really badly about that because I did not know who had done it. The book that I kept my sayings in I used every-day for my other writing of letters. I used to just lay it around, not paying any attention that others were paying attention to me and what I did. I was not going to sweat the situation because I was on my way home. My cards served their purpose. Maybe the inmates needed them more than I did because they still had to be locked up, and they had to make a living. Two and a half more weeks and counting. The closer it got for me to get out, the more scared it seemed like I got. I knew I would cry when I left because I 'm a big cry baby. Nevertheless, they were all going to be happy tears.

I was selling cards up to a week before my release. I finished selling my Father's Day cards, I sold fifty of them. I was selling two for one. The ladies thought that really was a bargain; I even gave some away to my best customers. If it had not been for some of my customers buying four to five cards from me a week, I do not know how I would have survived because I was not getting that much money from home. *God is good and worthy to be praised* all the time because He had my back the entire time I was locked up. I had run out of everything. All of my supplies were gone including the plastic that made my cards unique. See, I have been talented all my life and did not know it. The inmate who I was getting the plastic from had gone home a month before me, and she tried to stock me up on plastic and other materials that she was getting for me, and she did a very good job. The plastic lasted me up to my last days. I did not have any complaints. I had gotten tired of making cards; home was on my mind day and night then. I was trying to prepare myself mentally for my big day.

I had six days and a wake-up until my release. A wake-up mean that I will leave that morning. I started feeling anxiety. A few days prior, I was alone in my room. I was just sitting on the bed thinking about freedom, where I come from, when I first started my incarceration time, and all the things I had been through the past three years of my life. I just started crying. Tears were running down my face. I had to get control of myself. It was a good feeling to know I was about to walk out of these gates after so many years. It was almost like a fantasy. I approached the end of my sentence, having only three days and a wake up before I'd walk out a free lady. Some inmates lost their spirit. They felt they had no one to turn to, so they turned to drugs, and they said that was the first thing they were going to do when they got out. Others of the inmates were a total "wipe out," meaning she talked very negatively, and did not want to do anything with their lives when living the intuition, but there was hope for the hopeless. Like I said a million times before, God is there. Some cannot get away from their chronic decease and criminal behavior. Others never learned from their mistakes and they keep returning into the system. I wanted to get out and put this terrible experience behind me. For those who never learn, the final result is usually death.

I had started getting this very nervous feeling, a feeling that I knew would be hard for me to succeed in life and to get onto my feet; that was my biggest fear, *false evidence appearing real.* I knew I had to keep God at the head of my life and continue to let Him lead the way for me because every time I tried to lead my own life, I messed up. He would certainly show me the right way. I had started taking two Dimetapp's every other night to help me sleep. The white shirt lieutenant Mr. Williams at the prison who I had a very strong crush on the last past two years finally told me that we have to get together. He knew that I was about to leave. I was to go home on a Friday. What I did not know was that he was really lying. He would not be around to see me off since he had Fridays off. He told me he wanted to talk with me. He assured me that he wanted to give me his phone number or some other way for me to contact him after I was released. He was scared of losing his job I guess. That never turned into anything. When I told him I was going to attempt to write a book, he laughed at me and said we all have ups and downs in life and laughed at something I took very seriously. He was just so negative toward me. I did not like that at all. Even when I told him that I was thinking about becoming a drug counselor or something in that field, he laughed and said that everyone here in prison wants to be a drug counselor. There was no reinforcement from him. *I wish he could see me now.* He was putting me down and hurt my feelings even when I was considering being his clerk.

Everyone in population knew that I was leaving on Friday. They were standing around making excuses about paying me what they had owed me for making the cards for them. It six inmates owed me money when I left NEPRC. One of the inmates owed me for two weeks. She knew she could never get anything from me. Thus, she got a free card. I had stopped doing business with her because she did not pay me.

I had talked to Mom on the telephone. She told me that an old man friend of mine, John Dale, called her and asked if it was about time for me to come home. Mom told him it was time and what day I was to be released. He was talking very negatively to my mother about me such as she should get me a bible and leave all those no good men alone. He added, "She needs to stop smoking and drinking." He was an elderly man. The only reason he had stopped smoking and drinking was because he had so many health problems. I told my mother that I did not want to hear that kind of talk from him or anyone else. I had just finished doing three years; it was hell there to me, and I did not need to come out to hear someone preaching to me about what I should and should not have done. I think I had changed. God had opened my eyes as I had told my mother. She said she had seen a big change in me. John also asked my mom if he could come to the house on that Friday to see me. She told him "No," thank God. I was so glad she told him that. His talking down to me would have caused me to cuss him out and send him on his merry little way. Besides, he pretended that he had wanted to come to visit me and help me out the time while I was locked up. I do not know what was stopping him because he always did things for me when I was on the street. He also was a big liar as well. He owed my mom $150 dollars for five years, and she never got it. Not one time in the three years that I was locked up did he try to reach out to me to see if I had changed my ways or not. He just wanted to assume I was the same old wild Jean.

Then I was taking four Dimetapp's a day toward the end of my time. They weren't working. I still could not sleep like I wanted to. I was too excited and nervous at the same time about going home. I found myself smoking more cigarettes than I usually did; my nerves were getting the best of me.

The inmates started asking me questions like who was I going to live with. When was I coming back to see them? That was a very negative statement/question, but that is what they do, and their mentality was no larger than that, and so many ladies do return. I felt none of the questions were their business, and that is what I told them. If it were the Lord's will, He would keep me strong and positive and enlighten me when things or trouble headed my way. What I did not know then is that I still was not ready to change, I still wanted to do my own thing.

CHAPTER THIRTEEN

Being Released from Prison After three years

My last day was very stressful I was running around, checking with the necessary faculty members to make sure that I was ready to start school in September after leaving. I wanted to know what I had to do and get the necessary telephone numbers for future reference to contact faculty members at the prison. I also had to meet with Ms. Millie, the head of the "Start over Program." This organization helped in any way they could once I got back into society. I had signed up for this program some time ago. They were supposed to contact me three months in advance before I left. Ms. Millie had said that her company had many cutbacks; she was doing a lot of extra work, however, she stated she had not forgotten about me.

My roommate, Debbie, and I got into a small argument. It really was nothing, but she wanted to be noxious, and she got loud on me. Another roommate Joan, stepped in and said, "All right, you two!" Debbie is a hypochondriac anyway; she whines constantly about one thing or the other all the time. I kept on saying "Lord, have mercy--- thank God I'm out of this crazy place." Debbie calls herself a Christian.

She was the biggest hypocrite I knew. She had the nerve to always walk around with her Bible in her hand. My roommates were supposed to cook dinner for me my last night with them. By this time I did not care about the dinner. Debbie had angered me. Joan was the peacemaker in the room. She asked who was going to prepare the food and who was going to cook; Debbie and I did get the meal together after all. I still did not have much to say to her after that, the rest of the night. Before the yard had closed, I went to find the lady to arch my eyebrows. She did a really good jog. In the meantime, while I was waiting for her, I was just sitting outside looking around the area where I had spent three years; I was looking at all the women. It seemed as if they were on an island all by themselves; I was listening to women on the line as we called it which was really the walk jog, calling each other "Bitches," and "Mother-fuckers" as was usual talk for them. Their language made me sick. In my mind I went back to 1992 when I had gotten sentenced. A few ladies hugged me and said, "Good luck; get out there and do the right thing."

My last night at NEPRC was unbelievable. I could not sleep, and I tossed and turned all night long. Then that next morning it was time for me to leave. The institution kept me seem like forever before they finally released me because they had to run all of these national wide checks and I had to get the little money I had coming for the three years of having being locked up.

I was released on July 1, 1995. My mother picked me up and took me home. I got home for the second time after three years. I did not really want to do anything at first but just enjoy being at home, and I was glad to see my dog, Terri. When I got home and got out of the car, she was in the backyard playing. I stood at the end of the drive- way and called her, "Terri, Terri." She came charging from the backyard to where I was and jumped up into my arms. She was so glad to see me, and I thought she had forgotten who I was. She wanted to lick my face; I let her because she was my baby.

First church family mom is the tallest in
back My Pleasant church of God

I finally got hooked up with the support group. Millie came to the house and met my mother. I had to fill out a lot of paperwork. She had stated that the group would be going to the movies, bowling and things like that. None of that happened, maybe due to the program cuts. I was very disappointed, and I did not want to participate in the program. I thought the program was not right, and I did not want anything to do with it. I left North East Re-Release Center July 1, 1995. I stopped writing on my book. I started writing again May 28, 2010. At the time I did not know four years later I would be going right back through the prison revolving door.

I got back into school. My GPA dropped below 2.0 because I got a D in a class. That instructor was to give me work over the summer so I would not get dismissed from school. I had a change to bring that D up to a C. My instructor was very interested in dating me, but I would not date him for a grade. I knew all he wanted was to have intercourse with me, and I wanted to have a relationship. I got kicked out of Cuyahoga Community College. That money I had to pay back because I could not get anything below a C because of my financial aid.

CHAPTER FOURTEEN

Back to Prison for a Year and Boot Camp

Here I go again. I caught a case in 1998, which was about three years after being released after doing three years. I was to get probation. A person never knows how court will turn out. Sometimes you are lied to. I had a sitting in judge. It was almost guaranteed that I would get probation. When I walked into the court- room and saw this other judge, I said it was planned that way. That judge gave me a year at Marysville Correctional. I said "Oh my God, not again." While riding down 271 in Cleveland, Ohio, heading to Maryville, Ohio, outside of Columbus, I just could not believe I was taking that ride again. Once I got there, everything was the same process. I was not proud of being back. I thought the prison was going to send me back home to North East Pre-Release Center (NEPRC). The prison did not. They made me do my entire year at what we called Maryville farm. I did not want to be there.

While in admission, this group of inmates would march every day in what looked like military uniforms. They were looking good. I wanted to know who they were and how to get into their group. The group was called "Boot Camp." They had meetings, trying to recruit members. There was a group starting every thirteen weeks. I went to the meeting to find out more about Boot Camp and how to join. Boot Camp was called "Camp Meridian" which was the first female boot camp in Ohio, opened September 25, 1995, with a capacity for fifty inmates. The boot camp staff was dedicated to maintain a balance of military style bearing with discipline, physical training with social programming, and education. The purpose of the program was to provide resources and direction to non-violent, women offenders, allowing them to take better control of their lives upon release from the program in prison. I told them at the meeting that I could not do a push up. I was told at the time that was ok because they would work with me. That was a lie. I went ahead and joined. One of the advantages was that the boot campers went home a little earlier. For me, it was four months.

Once in Book camp the Lt. started "dogging" the new ladies right away. We were lined up in the hall- way. They had some of the older boot campers who were about to graduate help us make it through the first day which caused me to feel like I was in hell. It was a very hot day in the summer, the lieutenants were "all in our faces" and wearing a hat like Smokey the bear, specking in our faces, and they kept telling us not to look at him. They had to train us. My class was sixty nine that started on December 8, 1999. We originally started off with thirteen ladies class 69 was the smallest class there was up to that point. By the time we graduated there were six of us.

My intentions of going into Boot Camp were for the discipline and structure which I thought I needed so badly. We were issued nice uniforms, boots, new balances running shoes, rain coats, underwear, bras and anything else we might have needed. We had to buy all personally items, but if a boot camper did not have money on her books they would give it to us from state pay which was once a month. Being in boot camp, we got paid a little more than regular inmates. We were not allowed to talk to general population inmates; we had to march everywhere we went. We ate by ourselves, and we ate first. We could not eat anything off of commissary but jolly rangers. You would have thought I would have lost weight, but I did not. We ate as much as we wanted. Being in prison, boot camp was a good program. The staff had thirteen weeks to try and help thirty- something women and get to the bottom of their problems. Every three weeks a new group of inmates came in because a group would be leaving, going to the second phase in Columbus. Ohio. The second phase to Boot Camp that was not told to us until we got into the program that was in Columbus at a big house called the Alvin House that hailed the Boot Campers and other women could go out and work in the community daily.

After my first three weeks in boot camp, I stole a white girl's tennis shoes. All I had to do was ask for a new pair when they gave me a bad pair and I did not say anything.

The girl reported someone had switched shoes with her everybody then said Williams have on a new pair of shoes. They knew I had done it but I would not say for a long time I thought I was going to get kicked out of boot camp. I was made to strip my bed, pack all my belonging in my duffer bag. They let me sit there all day thinking about what I had done. I was never taken to the hole. They wanted the inmates to finish the program. I still thought I was slick and no one would ever know. I had to have been half crazy to think I was going to get away with that. After sitting on an empty bunk all day I kept wondering when they were going to take me to the hold. I still had to do all activates as if it was a normal day I was so embarrassed. I made an ass hole of myself and I had gotten labeled as the theft. Later that evening I confessed that I had stolen the girls' shoes. Everybody knew I had done it they were just waiting on me to admit to it. Man or man when I did they smoked me seem like forever in our square where we line up for formation, I had to get my duffle bag to the square and pour everything out for all my boot camp sisters to come and look at because lieutenant said I might have some of their things. Then after that they took me in what we call the cage where two lieutenants was all in my face talking about me like a dog spiting all in my face with their Smokey the brown hats on. They told me stuff like Williams get a job and I said sir "I have worked all my life." They were saying a lot of not true things. We all had done wrong because if we had of not, none of us would had be in prison. I was crying so hard clear mucus was running out of my noise and I was wiping it with my hands. After all that they made me clean up all my mess where they had make me dump out all my belonging. I was crying so hard. No one said a word to me. After all that I had to wear a white jump suit over my uniform to let everyone know I had done something wrong I was the only one who was in a white jumpsuit during my boot camp days. I had to take out all trash, run and get the doors for my boot camp sisters everywhere we went. Meals, commissary, doctor, anywhere on the farm I had to wear it all but Sundays when we went to church I did not have to wear it. I had to stay in the white jumpsuit for 30 days. I had to eat by myself and we ate first. We had to march to lunch turn a certain way, pick up our tray a certain way and if it was not correct, it would hold up the entire line until the boot camper got it correct if it took her too long and she could not get it right Lt use to tell her to go sit down there were three meals in a day therefore we got a lot of practice. I did not have to call cadets and I was glad I always wanted to call. When I came out of the jump suit Lt started calling on me to march the ladies and I was going to run them into the wall I got yelled at real bad sometimes I did half way ok until they stop calling on me. We could not talk during our marching some girls use to talk and Lt made us drop and give 10 pushups where ever we messed up at or somebody broke the rules we had to do push up and I went through the entire program without learning how to do a correct push up and they always smoked me for that. Sometimes the girls use to get down with me to try and help me sometimes the Lts allowed it and sometimes they made the girls get up because I guess they felt I should of learned how to do a pushup in all that time but I had told them that I never was able to do a push up in the beginning and I still got in trouble for it. They taught us in the program that there is no I in team. They made us stick together. After the tennis shoe incident, I was labeled the theft, and I did not like that.

We had to get passed the first phase. Eight of us graduated from Boot Camp, first phase. Craft got sent back to Marysville to finish her time out because of bad behavior, and other lies she had told on me while at the Alvin house. We marched everywhere we went as a group. We marched going into the community doing work at different places.

We worked at the fire station, we racked leaves, we planted flowers at nursing homes and other varies jobs around the Maryville community. When I graduated from Boot Camp, the entire gradating boot camper got sent to the beauty shop to get our hair done for graduation. Everyone looked so nice. I taught the ladies my favorite song, "We Come This Far by Faith" and led the song at graduation. My pastor Johnson attendant and my mother said she could not stand coming to the prison again. I told her that graduation would be different. I had never experienced anything like that before, and it was a very big deal to me. I had the best gift of all. None of the other inmates had anyone like that for them, and I did feel very special. Pastor Johnson was even at my graduation for my Bachelor's degree ceremony from Akron University. My own sister and her family did not come when I invited them. I made sure they saw all of my pictures. Sometimes, family doesn't care how they continually hurt you. They just look at the hurt that was done to them. Life goes on.

Before we went to the second phase, Columbus, Ohio, the head lady of the program came to talk to the boot campus ladies who would be going on to the second phase. At the time, there were thirteen of us. The head lady asked me a question. I was sitting in the back of the room not really caring about what she was saying because I was going to do what I had to do. She named me the happy boot camper. I knew the lieutenants had told her about me stealing those running shoes. The lieutenant had told the graduation class of sixty-nine that we had to write a letter of what Boot Camp had done for us and read it at graduation. It took me the longest to get my letter together. I had some of my boot camp sisters help me. We were about to leave Marysville Boot Camp. Today, I am so blessed and grateful that I did not get kicked out of Boot Camp. This is my letter below.

My Boot Camp Letter

I want to thank God who's Head of my life, my Lord and my savior. I also want to thank my family and pastor Another Johnson who supported me through these hard times of being locked up. When I went to Boot Camp, I thought I was getting a deal of ninety days and back home. Boy was I in for a rude awakening. God kept me focused on wanting to continue Boot Camp for the discipline and structure that I needed so badly. I knew I wanted to change my life; I just did not know how. I did not know what was wrong with me. I did not realize the importance of talking about things that had happened to me in my life that I had buried so deeply inside of me, and I was ashamed. Instead of me talking about my problems to someone, I held things inside of me, and I kept secrets. I just wanted to forget about them all. Over the years different issues were eating me up on the inside. It took me to go to Boot Camp to learn that the rape that happened to me had to come out and into the open. I felt people and family members would look at me differently and would not believe me since it happened to me when I was so young, and I acted out so badly. I wanted to take my anger out on the world. I thought people would not understand me. I thought no one cared about what happened to me or cared about my feelings. I had a lot of negative thoughts about how people viewed me as a person. I did not know it was all self-pity I was having. Boot Camp has helped me to realize how to dig deeply down within myself and soul search to open my heart up. This program has taught me to be humble and to know there is help for me if I want it. People do care about me because I care about myself. I am somebody who has to continue the rest of my life staying focused on the big picture. I have to give God all the glory because without Him who knows where I would be? God took me and is trying to make something beautiful out of my life, and He is not through with me yet. I do not know where He is taking me, but I am following Him for He is the answer. With God's help, "I can do all things through Christ who strengthens me." Philippians 4:13. I know today I have to address issues as they occur and get rid of all the old junk in my life in order for growth to take place. It is a process that I must follow. Boot Camp has made me a much stronger, motivated person. I've learned to adapt and overcome many situations. Thank You, God. Thank you, Boot Camp.

Pastor Anthony Johnson and I

Walking the stage me Doris Jean University of Akron 1995

My fellowship Church of God women group Sista to Sista, my
first lady front row second on left side and I fourth front row

Now we are on our way to Columbus, Ohio for the second phase
of Boot Camp. Then we go home from there if we finish the program
without getting into any trouble. If trouble occurs then that inmate
goes back to Marysville to finish her time. Ms. Schulte, the head lady,
looked up to me, and I did not know it at the time. I always am myself
that is the only way I know how to be, that is why I am called genuine.
By the time we graduated and left the Avis house, there were six (6)
of us who made it through the entire program. When we graduated
from the Alvin house in February 2000, the staff wanted us to put on a
graduation ceremony. My boot camp sisters wanted to do the same song
I had taught them. It was so true, God had kept each and every one of us
through the trials and tribulations of the Avis House and dealing with
all the ladies' attitudes, but we made it. I sang, "We Come This Far by
Faith," and the ladies were backing me up. Staff asked, "Who is that
singing?" They had to come behind their desks to listen to me because
they could not believe it was me. God has given me many talents, and
I wanted to use them all to His glory." I love singing to God because
there is power in words. When I walked out of the Alvin House, I did
not write another word for years. I had no desire to continue writing
at the time.

The night before I left the Alvin House I was feeling a little scared knowing I was leaving in the morning. I had to catch the Greyhound bus home. Everyone at Alvin House said I was looking very happy to leave, but inside of me I was scared to death. Boot Camp built up a lot of self-esteem in me. I do not act shy as I used to be.

Buddy and I

Doris Jean at Christmas

CHAPTER FIFTEEN

The Desire to Start Writing Again Working on My Degrees, Letters the New Year 2020

I started writing again on May 28, 2011. I had started talking to people, telling them that I had started writing my life story while I had been locked up. The more I talked about the situation, the more people encouraged me to pick my writing back up and try to get it published because I had a story to tell like so many people in the world have but everyone doesn't want to talk about his or her past to help another person. By me telling my story I have always said "If I could help one person that is a big accomplishment." I never know who I will help by what comes out of my mouth. During the ten (10) years of me not writing I had gained some of my goals as well as having had some set-backs

Years later I wanted to get back into college. However, I did not have the funds. I did not have the money to pay back financial aid in the amount of $800 dollars and I had no means of ever getting the money so I thought. I had to totally depend on God. I never gave my dream up. I did not know how, when, where things were going to happen for me, but I knew one day I was going to be allowed to go back and attempt to get my degree.

I went to Cuyahoga Community College to talk to the counselors to find out what I had to do to get back into college to attempt to get my Associate's Degree. At that time they had come out with grade forgiveness that was a blessing for me because I was fighting to get my GPA back up to a 2.0. I needed a fresh start. The counselor told me I had to write a letter stating what was different in me from back then to now. I wrote the letter. Then I had to have the letter checked by my English tutor Ken Cash who is still today one of my mentors He help me check for misspelled words, run-on sentences, sentence structure and to make sure it was appropriate for the situation of making sure I got back into college. I felt that was a one shot deal at least that is how I was approaching the situation. The letter was in my favor because it would not have hurt me. It would have only helped me back in college. With the grade forgiveness, a lot of my bad grades would come off from when I was in college acting as if it were a playground. I did get the grade forgiveness which it put my GPA at 2.0 because I was at a 1.80. Now I had to come up with the $800 dollars, and I did not know how that was going to happen until my mother's best friend Sister Mother Chappell who was also a minster, the oldest member at our church who was a retired school teacher as well, she asked me about my school situation, and I told her that I did not have that kind of money. She said she did. She gave me a check for the $800 dollars that got me back into Community College, and it was not a loan. I cried because she did not have to do that for me. No one else would have done that, I really do not believe. God had been with me all my life and I have had favor all my life and I did not know it. Yes, I am special. Like my oldest sister Ola use to tell me that God saw her finish college and He would do the same for me. "He did it for me" she said, and "He will do the same for you and others". It takes persistence, dedication, being hungry for knowledge, and wanting a better life. I wanted all that because I felt that an education was the only way out, and even with a degree, life would be hard for me because of my felonies. I have to give back and help others.

I graduated from Cuyahoga Community College. One of my

instructors convinced me to continue going on to get a bachelor's degree. At the time I did not want a bachelor's. All I wanted to do was work. My past was so terrible until I knew I needed some letters behind my name to get a decent job. I was also told by the same instructor as well as one of my chemical dependent counselors who said that I would be ok as long as I did not get into any more trouble. I believed them so I thought. I was about to file for my Parton forgiveness with the government, I had a pretty good chance of getting it because I had over ten years clean without being caught doing anything wrong. That went out the window.

I got into the social work program at Cleveland State it was a task to get into the program but I was a fighter. There were still a lot of ups and downs. I only knew social work was to help people to find themselves, and I needed to find out who I was. I loved my classes because in the beginning of my career the class had to tell problems that were going on within us. Some people did not want to talk at first until I started opening up telling about how embarrassed I was with my life and how embarrassing my family was of me. At the time I did not see where I was hurting my family at all. I was totally in the dark for many, many years. I was still maintaining good grades for over a year. The further I got into my classes and my education, I knew either I had to stop smoking dope, or I was going to fall and I fail. I knew something was going to stop me. I never thought it would be me catching a case going back to jail. I caught the new and last case April 2012; that was one of the most embarrassing moments in my life. Drugs are a disease. I have seen some of the best people go down because of drugs. I stayed in the county jail in downtown Cleveland for over thirty days. At the time no one in my family would help my man get me out on bond, and it took him time to raise the money. My bond was $10,000. I said, "Who did I kill?" The bond was so high because of my past record. I do not think things like that are fair because the judge knew I had not been in any trouble for ten years I was doing a lot of positive and good things in my life. How could God continue blessing me when I was doing wrong? In and out, in and out of things thinking I was slick. I had been in and out of Cocaine Anonymous (CA) and Narcotic Anointments (NA) I did not like NA because the members thought they were better than other. I had gotten very involved in CA. I was the chairperson once. My home group got me business right away. I had a sponsor. All the men were after me it seemed like because I was build up nicely. I did not know that those people were just as sick as I was in the program. A guy who was interested in me, he and I hung out a lot, and he helped me to get my first year in without doing anything. I thought he really was the one I was going to be with long turn. The relationship did not last for a year after I got my first year in. What I have learned over the years that people are put in one's life for a reason, a season or a life time.

I thought I was getting my life back together but in the back of my mind, I knew something was going to happen. I could not stop smoking dope. That is a disease that is hard to get off of. I knew I had a lot of problems but I did not know how to fix them. As time went on I started getting better and better so I thought. I got the big head telling myself "OH, I can do this, oh, I got this." I had stopped going to meetings and had stopped being active in the program of CA. I was in college, and I had to continue my classes. What I did not know is without recovery, there is nothing. After two years at Cleveland State, I started using drugs again, off and running, chasing that white ghost. I thought no one knew I was back on drugs because no one said anything to me. I thought I was keeping my looks up, but my fingertips stayed burned, and I tried to hide that but my man Buddy and others knew and no one said anything to me. My man did not ever leave me, and I loved him so much for staying with me. He took me to rehab and stayed by my side the entire time. In May of 2012 when the semester and my case were over I got put on probation and I went back into rehabilitation for in house treatment for ninety days. I had a lot of trouble with some of the women at the treatment center. I was in treatment with hookers, hoes who worked the streets, addicts, etc. Everyone was court ordered but me. I had gotten tired of crack, and I knew my life was better than that. First, I went to detox at Stella Maris on the west side of Cleveland because I was an alcoholic first before I ever thought about a drug. I stayed in Stella Maris for seven (7) days. After that, the facility found me a treatment center to go to which was Hitchcock recovery center for women locate on East 82 and Saint Clair Avenue. The first time they did not want to keep me because I had too many doctor appointments coming up. I was told to go home and take care of my business and then come back. I did not want to do that because I did not feel strong enough, and I felt I was going to use again if I went home, and that is exactly what I did. On April 27, 2016, I had been clean for four years. Life was hard for me to get into my field of social work or chemical dependent Counseling.

My two sisters behind mom, sister, Ola passing,
brother and cousins in background.

I wonder if anyone will cry at my funeral.

For the third time I got my Chemical Dependence Counselor Assistance license (CDCA). For the first time I actually used it as I was doing my internship at Community Action against Addiction (CAAA). I work with clients in group, helped with intake, did assessments, scan for the medical department and anything else I was asked to do by my clinical director Mary Bazie, I graduated with my Master's in Addiction counseling on April 26, 2019 from Grand Canyon Christian University in Phoenix Arizona. I was taking on line classes which were always a fear for me. My friend Darryl Jenkins and his family made me so welcome in Phoenix, him and I grew up in Cleveland Ohio at Mt Pleasant church of God when we were just children under the late Pastor George Suddeth who was Pastor Anthony Johnson Uncle.

Until my parents died, I never knew how much they loved me even though I felt my mother never showed love to me, however, she keep me clear and a roof over my head. As I look back and my parents are not with me now I know they did the best they could with very little education and money. I miss then more than ever. I now feel sometimes lost within me having no biology family or a relationship. I thank God for His grace and mercy because without his love where would I be. I came out of it and tried to make something beautiful of myself before it was too late, and anybody could do the same thing however, he or she has to really want it.

I finally received my part two of my CDCA for the first time. I got it on April 2020 and I did not know it, however, I knew it was time for it with the corona virus going on it was delayed. I have also just completed my certificate for life coaching on May, 2020. My girlfriend Nicole and I was planning a cruise to the Bahamas for four days on August 13, 2020. It got cancelled due to the coronavirus. I turned around and booked me on another cruise to the Bahamas on April 15, 2021. I hope and pray it do not get cancel. It got canceled I will try again for May or June 2021, my girlfriend Shelia Smith Roberson will be joining me. I went to a cruise to Jamaica about seven years ago and I had a ball.

The newest addition to my family. Amy the
mother and Kitty the daughter.

CHAPTER SIXTEEN

END OF 2019 and the BEGINNING OF 2020

The last three weeks of December, 2019 was a night mare for me. Starting with I got into two accident within six months, neither one was not my fault. The first accidents happen on June 15, 2019 and the second Friday December, 13 2019.

The first accident a young lady hit me in the rear knocking me into the car in front of me, I was sitting still because the lady in front of me could not make up her mind if she was going to keep straight or turn into the auto part store. I think the young lady was on the telephone because it was a delayed reaction of her hitting me, then she hit me hard. I did not know at the time how much damage she had done to my car, she ran and I followed her into an apartment complex which was down the street, I saw her in back of me at first, when I looked back up she was gone the people who saw the accident said to me she took off. The other lady said she was not hurt "Go get her." I went down the street where I saw her pull in at and I pulled right next to her, she did not know who I was I had my window down, she did not so I said to her "So you are just going to tear my car up and take off ."She finally recognized who I was and took off again down the street and I followed her until I wrote her license plate number down. She had no insurance, I stop following her and I turned that information into the police. My insurance company totalled my car. I still had a car note. I had to pay eleven hundred dollars to buy my car from my insurance company, then I had to get the car fixed on my own, that charge to fix my car was twenty-five hundred dollars. Mr. Mo fixed my car on E 79 Street, Chester Avenue in Cleveland Ohio. Since I was paying cash the body shop owner Mo worked with me. My 2015 Ford Focus was looking real good again. I was happy because it was looking like it did before it got hit and the good part about that was now I have no car note.

Three weeks after I got the car out the shop here comes the second accident. I was heading to my credit union, and never made it there. I was traveling straight down the street; this man was traveling at a high rate of speed trying to hurry up to get onto the freeway. I saw him and I tried to dodge him from hitting me when I was unsuccessful, he turned right into me, he hit me on my side and knocked me up onto the side walk. I was pended in the car. My head, neck and left leg was messed up. The accident could have been worse. I am still here to tell the story and able to add the last three weeks of 2019 into my book. It was a living hell for me, however the man who hit me was apologizing, and he just keep on apologizing to me that he was so sorry. I just keep on saying I just got my car fixed. I went to the hospital in an ambulance and he drove off. My car got towed away to the in-pound and I prayed to God that by the New Year I would be in a new car if it was His will and I was. The man kept on saying "I am going to call my insurance company right now." He did that by the time I got to the hospital his insurance company was calling me saying that they take full responsibly for the accident and did I need a renter car I said "Yes." His insurance company total my car a second time and I end up getting about 6 thousand dollars to get another car.

My friend Mo, who fixed my car the first time, had a partnership with some of his buddies who own a car lot dealership on Waterloo Road in Cleveland Ohio. Mo went on line to show me the Black KIA Sol and I trusted Mo he had told me that car was for me. I had looked at a Mazda 06 I liked that car I had a Mazda 3 before and the only thing about that car is that after a year or so it rusted real badly and I did not like that at all. I had told Mo about the car and he kept on telling me that the KIA SOL was a better car for me. I prayed, and I prayed hard for God to show me which car he wanted me in. The *KIA SOL* kept popping up over and over again in my face. When Mo took me to see the KIA they had it sitting out front. I asked Mo as we pulled into the lot "Was that it," he said "Yes" I said "Yes I want it, the small SUV was so pretty and it had my name all over it. I did not even want to test drive it. Mo made me.

I was in a renter car that was due back on December 31, 2019 by 3:00 if not I would have had to pay for two more days because they were closed on January 1, 2020. I called the car rental place to ask them if they had an office somewhere around Waterloo Road, come to find out they did it was an office between East 222 and East 260 Street off the freeway on Lakeland Boulevard that worked out for me. I told the renter company that I was buy a car and I would not make it to them by 3:00pm and it they could wait on me about 5 minutes, they said "Yes." I thank God that he allowed everything to go real smoothly. He allowed everything to work like clockwork.

After my birthday which was December 26 I brook my top partial mouth plate and I could not eat. I had a little money in the bank. My teeth broke on Saturday, that Monday morning I went back where I got my top plate made at; they made it in a day. It cost me three hundred twenty five dollars. I could eat once again. I was spending money that was supposed to be for my new car. I got my car on December 31, 2019 New Year Eve. It snowed so hard in Cleveland that day. New Year's Day, came in like a rose for me, I did not go out of the house. I was just thanking God for being so good to me.

January 2020 as the year moved on a lot of things were happening. The biggest thing this year this far was the cov19 virus. The city has been shut down about two months. Everyone was walking around with mask on their face, stores were closed down, restaurants, beauty shops, beauty supplies stores, nails shops, bars and a lot others. Boy- O- Boy, I needed my nails and hair done so badly.

When the virus first started friends of mind and I were heading to Detroit Mi. I had not been there in 20 years or better. Regardless, I still had a nice time at the hotel which was downtown Detroit. I walked about 6 blocks sight-seeing and stopping in stores buying things. I went out one night with my friends and they went out two nights I told then it was too much for me so I hung around the hotel watching movies. My friend's family in Detroit was very nice to me, I enjoyed them. We left Cleveland Friday afternoon arriving in Detroit about 6 pm and we stayed until Monday afternoon. I did not get to see a lot of things that I wanted to because so much was close or closing. The night club was jammed packed.

May 15, 2020 the governor just opened some things back up in the city. I feel it might be too early, I feel things will never go back to the way it was. We are still today practicing safe distance of supposedly 6 feet some people just do not want to follow the rules. I think this is going to be the new way of life of wearing mask on our face. By mermonal day just around the corner people are just not following the rules, they are doing what they want to do and I am looking for the city to be shut down again or a lot more people are going to die. I ended up having a good day which was unexpected friends and I were playing cards, and eating chicken all day. I needed that really to relax because I do not do anything anymore.

Cleveland State University
engagedlearning™

Office of Judicial Affairs
Department of Student Life

August 11, 2014

Ohio Chemical Dependency Professional Board
Vern Riffe Center
77 South High Street, 16th Floor
Columbus, OH 43215

Re: Doris Williams

Dear Licensing Board:

It is my pleasure to serve as a reference on behalf of the above-named individual, Ms. Doris Williams, who is applying for licensure as a Chemical Dependency Counselor. I have known Ms. Williams for two (2) years. I met her when she was a student at Cleveland State University and served as her mentor.

Ms. Williams is pursuing a degree in Social Work and her interest in the field is based on some of her own life experiences. As a Social Worker, Ms. Williams' goal is to work as a Chemical Dependency Counselor with chemically dependent women as her target population.

Ms. Williams will be a valuable asset to the profession. She has a good insight to the problems that confront chemically dependent persons, has excellent interpersonal skills, is knowledgeable about the field and when she completes her degree, Ms. Williams will be able to apply in practice what she has learned in theory. Ms. Williams' academic progress is good and I think she will be successful as a Chemical Dependency Counselor.

If there are any specific questions or concerns, please contact me at 216-523-7209.

Sincerely,

Valerie Hinton Hannah
Assistant Dean of Students/Judicial Affairs Officer

Mailing Address: 2121 Euclid Avenue, SC 319 • Cleveland, Ohio 44115-2214
Campus Location: Student Center, Room 319 • 2121 Euclid Avenue • Cleveland, Ohio
(216) 687-2048 • Fax (216) 687-5441

222

Letter Of Reference For Doris Williams

I have known Ms Williams for 2 years as a student in the Social Work Cleveland State University. The time I have known Ms Williams have opportunity to assess her strengths and weaknesses.

Ms Williams is responsible, hard working, secure, eager to learn and Social Work Code of Ethich and Values.

Please feel free to call me in my office and Cleveland State Universit questions.

3/18/14

Sincerely,
Julius L. Simmon
Telephone: 216-!
523-7472

ncba

ˇ 7b» National Caucus and Cantor on Black Apnq. Inc.

£2200 Fairhill Road Cleveland, Ohio
44120 216.721.9197
216.721.1251 Fax

To Whom It May Concern;

I am pleased to provide a reference letter for Doris Williams.

I have worked with. Doris as a participant with the NCBA/SCSEP (National Caucus and Center on Black Aging, Inc. Senior Community Service Employment Program).

Doris would be an asset to any organization with her enthusiastic, dedicated and reliable work habits. She often does not need guidance or supervision, but willingly accepts it when offered. She is consistently successful in improving her skills and she work hard to do so. She is definitely a leader rather than a follower.

Sincerely

* 4 JEWISH FAMILY SERVICE" .ASSOCIAfION OF CLEVELAND
40 JFSA CLEVELAND 29125 CHAGRIN BLVD., PEPPER PIKE. OHIO
44122 ! 216.292.3999 JFSA-CLEVELAHD.ORG

July 31, 2019
Doris Williams

To Whom It May Concern: I

As an Employment Specialist I have had the pleasure of working with Doris for almost four years, since August of 2015. During that time she has accomplished a great deal, from obtaining and maintaining a job appropriate to her skills, to earning a Master's degree to inspiring others to achieve their goals. During that time she, demonstrated her reliability and professionalism consistently.

Doris is proficient in systems, computers, protocols, but she truly excels in her interpersonal skills. Especially in populations with serious challenges she is able to listen attentively and empathetically but appropriately and then lead them to services that best, meet their needs. She reminds me of a story about a life coach. The client is in a hole. Various people come by offering help or advice but the person remains in the hole. Then the life coach comes by and immediately jumps in. The persoacries, "Why did you jump in? Now we're both stuck here." But the life coach says calmly, "No, I've been here before and I know the way out." That is Doris exactly.

I would recommend her for any position she is determined to have, or for any program she is seeking, as over time she has demonstrated that her tenacity, resilience, intelligence and perseverance will ensure she will achieve her goals.

If there is any further information I can provide, please contact me, at the address below or at imagnus@ifsa-cleveland.org or by phone at 216-378-3568.

Sincer
ely,

'Joli Magnus Employment Specialist

Learning Commons and Academic Support Services
Metropolitan Campus | 2900 Community College
Avenue | Cleveland, Ohio 44115-3196
216-987-4292 | Fax 216-987-4404

July 25, 2019 **where futures begin"**

To Whomever This May Concern:

Please consider this communication as a letter of reference for Ms. Doris Williams.

As an instructional specialist at Cuyahoga Community College, I have tutored Ms. Williams in English since her enrollment many years ago. Since graduating from Tri-C, she has visited me at Tri-C on several occasions throughout her continued education.

Without exaggeration, after forty years of tutoring, Ms. Williams is probably the most industrious student with whom 1 have worked.

Moreover, she has consistently shown immense enthusiasm for her studies and actual working experiences. She is also intelligent and insightful. Ms. Williams is exceedingly concerned with following professional guidelines and displays good judgment.

During her academic studies at Tri-C, she was a guest on an episode entitled "Post-Prison Blues" of *WesTVmos,* a televised series broadcast over Tri-C monitors and two cable television networks, a show which I co-produced and conducted the interview. The interview regarded her prison stretches, inmate status but mainly results of having been incarcerated. I selected Ms. Williams to appear on the show. She was an excellent guest.

i I think that Ms. Williams would be a superb candidate for serving as a life coach because she is a genuine individual who relates[1] well to other people.

I think that Doris Williams would be a fine addition to an employer.

Sincerely yours,

Kenneth P. Cash
Instructional Specialist - English
Ph: 216-987-4326
E-mail: kenneth.cash@tri-c.edu
Cuyahoga Community College

)[Community^ Action Against Addiction
5209 Euclid Avenue • Cleveland, Ohio 44103 • Phone 216.881.0765 • Fax
216.361-7216 Gladys V. Hall, Chief Executive Officer

April 23, 2019

To whom it May Concern,

This letter is written on behalf of Ms. Doris Williams and is meant to serve
as a reference. I have known Doris for about a year and have worked with her
as an instructor, as she was assigned to our agency as an intern. Ms. Williams
is an open and eager student and I am sure this will translate into any work
placement to which she is assigned.

Ms. Williams learned the Group Process while here, she did screening
for new admissions, made follow-up phone calls to clients seeking treatment
and to those who were AWOL from treatment, and she was able to engage
clients into the counseling process. She was just learning how to work in the
individual counseling arena as her assignment here ended and I confident she
will learn this skill also with proper instruction and guidance.

I am hopeful this letter is helpful In your decision to hire her as I think
she could be an asset to any agency which hires her. Please feel free to contact
me I can assist further in this matter.

)
eTKSSA, LISW-S,'tiepC-CS, Clinical Director.

~~Mary Bazl~~   Sincerely,

For the young people in the world, never give up on your hopes and dreams. The sky is the limit. You can do anything you put your mind to do. Do not let anybody tell you what you cannot do. Either they are jealous, and do not want you to advance in life for whatever reason. There are many haters in life. As long as you keep a positive attitude on life, keep on asking questions, and God will send you your angels in life. Stay teachable, be hungry for knowledge. I never knew there was so much knowledge in reading because I could not read or write that well, and I did not understand what I had read. Today, I am much better in my reading and writing. Do not wait until you get my age because it will be much harder on you. Most people are afraid to do what I have done in life, but God was right by my side through it all, and He is still there leading and guiding me along my journey. He is not done with me yet, and I know that. I thank God for all His many *Blessing.*

For the older adult and the ex-con, I am an ex-con myself. I thought no one would understand me, but they did because God knew my pain and all of my burdens which I was carry around with me for years. I have been there and done that. Stop feeling sorry for yourself. Get off your buttocks, and keep on trying. I guarantee that in a years' time, you will start seeing better results in your life. Keep God as Head of your life on your side, and watch Him do His work. He did it for me, and He will do it for you as well. I hope and pray my words will help somebody because so many people have helped me. May God bless and keep you all strong. I want to thank all my readers, friends and family who supported my book. You can reach me at dorispalmer11@yahoo.com

My mother, brother Michael and I

My brother Michael Williams who died January 23rd, 2021 about 8 or 9 PM. I got the call at 9 PM while at work. He was rushed to the hospital and died of a heart attack. That was a very hurting ordeal. I didn't know he had been sick, after he had gotten out of the Navy many years ago. He made his home in Halifax Nova Scotia Canada. He worked as a Chemical Dependency Councilor working with disabled men and women. He had told me that there were no one else who could do anything with some of the clients but him to calm those clients down. He was always called on to handle the most difficult situations. Rest in peace my younger brother.

Printed in the United States
by Baker & Taylor Publisher Services